A
PARENT'S
GUIDE
TO
WILLS
&
TRUSTS

DON SILVER
Attorney-at-Law

■

ADAMS-HALL PUBLISHING
LOS ANGELES

Requests for such permissions should be addressed to:

Adams-Hall Publishing, PO Box 491002
Los Angeles, CA 90049-1002

No patent liability is assumed with respect to the use of the information contained herein. While every precaution has been taken in the preparation of this book, the publisher and the author assume no responsibility for errors or omissions. Neither is any liability assumed for damages resulting from the use of the information contained herein.

Library of Congress Cataloging-in-Publication Data

Silver, Don
    A Parent's Guide to Wills & Trusts
        p.   cm.
    Includes index.
    ISBN 0-944708-40-4
    1. Wills-United States-Popular Works. 2. Trusts and trustees-
    United States-Popular Works. 3. Inheritance and succession-
    United States-Popular Works. I. Title. II. Title: A Parent's
    Guide to Wills & Trusts.
KF755.Z9S486 1992
346.7305'4--dc20
[347.30654]   92-815
                                                                CIP

Cover Design by Robert Steven Pawlak

Adams-Hall books are available at special, quantity discounts for bulk purchases for sales promotions, premiums, fund-raising or educational use. For details, contact: Special Sales Director, Adams-Hall Publishing, PO Box 491002, Los Angeles, CA 90049-1002 (1/800-888-4452).

Printed in the United States of America
10 9 8 7 6 5 4 3 2
First printing 1992   Printed on recycled paper

To Charles, Emily, Ralph and Marilyn

and especially to

Susan and Charlie

Disclaimer

All of the names and situations in this book are hypothetical and the resemblance to anyone's actual situation is purely coincidental.

This book is intended to provide accurate information. It is not intended, however, to render any legal, tax, accounting or other professional advice or services. You should therefore use this book as a general guide only. In addition, this book contains information that was available only up to the time of printing. Laws do change with some frequency.

That's why you must discuss your estate planning with a qualified attorney before relying on the information you may find here or anywhere else.

CONTENTS

continued

INTRODUCTION

WHY

YOU

SHOULD

READ

THIS

BOOK

You love your children more than anything.

You would do anything for them. But *have* you?

If something happened to you, would their fate be cast to the wind? Or, have you made all the necessary legal arrangements to:
- select a guardian to raise your children
- leave enough to raise and educate your children
- meet your child's special needs and situations
- avoid family disputes
- do special planning as a divorced parent
- do special planning where you have children from a prior marriage
- choose a guardian, executor and trustee to manage your assets
- make sure you don't accidentally shortchange a child
- leave money to adult children as well as grandchildren
- reduce attorney's fees and save death taxes?

Do you know
- how to avoid probate
- when to set up a living trust
- how to handle incapacity and death-bed situations
- the seven biggest myths about wills and trusts?

Part of the responsibility of being a parent is to deal with our own passing. I've seen the personal and financial pain caused to families who put off handling a will or trust.

A **Parent's Guide to Wills & Trusts** is designed to make the process of completing your will or trust easier and to guide you through the main decisions and concerns you need to address as a parent or grandparent.

As an attorney who restricts his practice to drafting wills and trusts and handling probates, I've dealt with these issues on a professional basis. I've also dealt with them personally. At age 32, I lost my first wife. At age 40, I lost my father. One year later I became a father myself.

The topics in this book are all broken up into bite-size questions and answers that are easily digested by you. The detailed index makes it easy for you to look up what's on your mind.

This book can help you in three ways. First, it can help you find out what might happen to you and your loved ones if you did nothing.

Second, this book may help you save tens or even hundreds of thousands of dollars in income and death taxes and costs as well as save your family the kind of aggravation that has no price tag.

Third, this book will open your eyes to new possibilities. You'll take part in a creative process to discover the right solutions for you.

In this book I'm striving, to the extent possible, to take into account individual differences and situations. Since all people and situations are unique, however, it is impossible to provide information in a book that applies equally to every parent and to every family. The "rules" set forth in this book are generalizations. *Unless you consult with an attorney, you cannot know whether your particular circumstances fit the rule or the exceptions to the rule.*

This is definitely *not* a self-help or do-it-yourself book. It is not intended to be a substitute for professional advice. You are doing yourself and your loved ones no favor if you try to prepare your own will or trust or do your own estate planning. This is a very complex area of law that requires the professional assistance of an attorney and sometimes also a CPA and life insurance agent.

The effort you make now in understanding the key concepts in this book will better prepare you when you meet with your estate planning professionals. You'll feel more comfortable with this complex area of law and you'll be in a better position to make those critical decisions affecting the future of your loved ones. And, you'll have that special peace of mind that comes from getting your will or trust in order.

Don Silver

PART ONE

THE
SEVEN
BIGGEST MYTHS
ABOUT
WILLS
&
TRUSTS

MYTH #1

Joint tenancy is always the best way for parents and children to hold title together to avoid probate.

QUESTION: I want to avoid a probate upon my death. I've heard that I can avoid probate by putting my adult children on the title to my house as joint tenants. Is that a good idea?

Maybe, maybe not. You must understand that joint tenancy means more than just a way to avoid probate in the event of your death. Holding assets with your children as joint tenants also has an effect while you are alive.

If your children become joint tenants with you, they are co-owners of your house while you are alive. Putting aside some of the technical gift tax, income tax, property tax and death tax issues, let's just talk about the financial risk you are taking when you hold title as joint tenants with your children.

If one of your children has a business that goes under, your child's creditors may go after your child's portion of the house *while you are alive*. If one of your children is at fault in a car accident where your child's car insurance is not enough to cover the damage, the injured party may go after your child's portion of the house *while you are alive.*

So, if you want to avoid probate *and* also avoid being responsible for your adult children's debts and actions, you should talk to your attorney about setting up a living trust instead. That way you'll be able to sleep at night and not be your children's keeper for the rest of your life. Although living trusts are more fully described later, for right now, you just need to know that a living trust is in essence a substitute for a will that allows your successors to avoid the probate court after your death.

The bottom line is that while a technique such as joint tenancy may be good for one purpose (e.g., avoiding probate), it can have other, unintended effects that could be a disaster.

Also, if you hold title with your children as joint tenants and you and your children pass away simultaneously, such as in a car accident or a plane crash, the house may go through several probates, yours and your children's. So, joint tenancy may not even give you the benefit of avoiding probate, and it will eliminate your ability to control who inherits portions of the house from your children's estates.

If you have minor children, all of the above applies and even more so, since there may be additional complications in transferring assets or getting loans on assets owned by minors.

HINT: If your goal is to avoid probate upon your death, look into setting up a living trust instead of holding title as joint tenants with your adult or minor children. See your attorney for the right way for you to hold title.

I signed my will so long ago that it's not good anymore.

QUESTION: It has been over thirty years since my husband and I signed our last wills. Our kids were so small then. I guess the wills aren't good any more since so much time has gone by. I sure hope so because in the wills, we named my brother as the executor and that's the last thing we would want now. Would our wills still be valid even though the paper has yellowed through the years?

Yes. A vintage wine may mellow and an old will may yellow, but only one of them may be easy to swallow.

HINT: Run, don't walk, to your attorney if your will or trust is out of date.

Thank goodness my ex-spouse cannot inherit my assets.

QUESTION: My husband and I recently divorced. It was not a pleasant divorce. We have two grown children. I just signed a new will eliminating my former spouse as the beneficiary and instead naming our two children. Our children are unmarried and have no children of their own. I feel so much better knowing my ex-spouse can never inherit my assets. Have I covered all my bases?

Probably not. Consider the following scenario: If you pass away, your two children will inherit from you. What happens if one of them then passes away without leaving a will or trust and without having a spouse or child of their own? State law may say that your child's closest relative, the child's father (your ex-spouse) will inherit the child's assets (including what your child inherited from you). Also, what if your children were to sign a will or trust naming their father as the beneficiary of the assets inherited from you?

HINT: Instead of leaving assets outright and in the pockets of your children, you might want to put some strings on the assets such as creating trusts for your children.

The trusts could allow your children to benefit from your assets but control who would ultimately inherit whatever is left over after your children pass away.

Talk to your attorney about how such trusts could be written. Keep in mind that it will cost more now in attorney's fees to have trust provisions written as compared to leaving your assets outright to your children. Also, there will be greater legal and accounting costs through the years after your death in connection with such trusts for your children.

If your worst nightmare is the possibility of your ex-spouse inheriting your hard-earned assets, please discuss this matter with your attorney. After you obtain the needed information, you'll be able to make the right decision (and sleep at night).

To make the right decision, you'll need to balance the costs associated with a trust, the size of your estate and how likely it will be for your ex-spouse to inherit under these circumstances.

By signing a new will, I will automatically override the beneficiaries named on my life insurance, IRAs and retirement plans.

QUESTION: I am a widower. Years ago I named my brother as the beneficiary on my life insurance, IRAs and retirement plans. That's all I really have. Now I don't want my brother to receive those benefits when I die. I want my daughter to get the benefits. I recently signed a new will naming my daughter as the only beneficiary of my estate. Should I bother to take the time to fill out new beneficiary forms or does my new will automatically protect my daughter?

Usually beneficiary designations have a life of their own outside of your will or trust. In general, your will or trust will *not* override the beneficiary designations naming your brother. So, why leave any doubt as to your intentions?

You'll want to fill out new designation forms as soon as possible, naming your daughter as the primary beneficiary (be sure to fill in a secondary or contingent beneficiary designation, too).

HINT: Always keep your beneficiary designations up to

date to reflect your current intent.

If the beneficiaries under your will or trust differ from those selected in other designations (e.g., life insurance, retirement plan and IRA beneficiary designations), you should make it clear in your will or trust that this has been done intentionally. This will avoid costly fights and help keep family harmony.

The reason it's important to complete a secondary or contingent beneficiary is that in many cases the benefits will be paid to your estate if your primary beneficiary dies and you haven't named a second choice. There are two main problems with these benefits going to your estate. First, the benefits become subject to attorney's fees and delays that might otherwise have been avoided. Second, if the benefits are paid to your estate, you may have converted an asset that was exempt from creditor's claims to one that may be taken by creditors.

Since the laws are the same everywhere in the U.S., a will or trust will work the same everywhere.

QUESTION: I just received a promotion and my wife and I will be moving out of state. From all of my job-hopping and the soft real estate market, we now own houses in three different states. Our other main asset is stock. We're dividing our assets between our children and grandchildren. Do we need to have our wills reviewed or are the laws the same every-where?

There are certain federal tax laws that apply across the U.S.

However, the laws for wills, trusts and inheritance are *not* identical in all of the states. And, there are different state income tax and property tax laws across the country.

So, what might have made sense in one state might need to be changed in another state.

You are leaving the three houses and stocks to your children and grandchildren. One state, for example, might allow property taxes to remain lower after your death only to the extent your children, and not your grandchildren, inherit the house. With this in mind, you might change your estate plan to allocate the house in that one state only to your children and a compensating amount of the houses in other states or stocks just to your grandchildren to take advantage of this property tax benefit.

HINT: When you arrive in your new state, you should have an estate planning attorney review your entire estate plan to make sure it will produce the results you want in every state in which you have assets.

Last-minute gifts by terminally ill persons always save taxes.

QUESTION: I am very ill. I have one child, a son who's 44. I have some stocks that I bought many years ago for $20,000. They are now worth $120,000. This is the only asset of any value I've ever had. After I die, my son will be selling the stocks to get the cash. Will my son pay less to the IRS in death taxes if I give the stocks to him before I die? I assume for income tax purposes it doesn't matter whether he gets the stocks now or after my death.

Actually, in this case, the result is the reverse of what you think it would be. Due to the value of your assets, there would be no federal gift tax or death tax whether your son received the stocks now or after your death. And, if your son did *inherit* from you (rather than receive the stocks now as a gift), he would pay *less* in *federal income tax* from a sale of the stocks.

Your question brings up the relationship among three types of taxes: death tax, gift tax and income tax (see page 27 for definitions of "death tax" and "gift tax").

First, let's look at the federal death tax and federal gift tax consequences of your situation.

With certain exceptions, every U.S. citizen or permanent resident can give away up to $600,000 in assets during one's lifetime or at death and pay *no* federal gift tax or federal death tax. This $600,000 exemption amount may be used during one's lifetime to exempt gifts from gift tax. Whatever is unused during one's lifetime is available at one's death.

So, for federal gift or federal death tax purposes, it will not matter whether you give your son the stocks now or if he inherits them from you after you are gone. Either way, you are well under the $600,000 exemption amount. If your estate were larger, last-minute gifts could save considerable death taxes (more about that later).

However, death taxes are not the only taxes to consider. If you give your son the stocks before you die, your son may end up paying more to the IRS in *income tax*. Why is this?

When you make a gift to someone, the person receiving the gift basically steps into your shoes for income tax purposes.

If your starting point (called your income tax basis) is $20,000 in this case and you give your son your stocks now, then when your son sells the stocks for $120,000 he has a gain of $100,000 (the $120,000 received for the stocks less the $20,000 you paid for the stocks). He has to pay income tax on the $100,000 gain.

How can your son legally avoid paying the federal income tax on the gain?

The rules are different for federal income tax purposes when your children (or grandchildren or anyone else) *inherit* from you at your death as compared to when you make a *gift* to them during your lifetime.

When your children inherit from you, the starting point for federal income tax gain or loss on a sale by them is *not* what you paid for the asset ($20,000 in this case), it's what it was worth when you died ($120,000 in this case).

So, for example, if the stocks were worth $120,000 when you died and your son sold the stocks for $120,000 after he *inherited* them from you, he would have *no gain for federal income tax purposes.* Thus, a tax savings of tens of thousands of dollars in income tax could result from you *not* making a gift during your lifetime.

There are other factors for you to discuss with your attorney, such as how to avoid a probate on assets that are inherited by children, what the state death tax and income tax rules and rates are where you live, what prior gifts you have made, the personal circumstances of your children, the kinds of assets you are thinking of giving to your children, and whether there are other estate planning tax factors to consider that might change the answer in your case.

On the bright side, there are several advantages to making a gift while you are still alive. First, you can remove assets from your taxable estate without any extra gift or death tax cost. Second, those assets that have been given away will avoid probate on your death. Third, the gifted assets may result in a lower death tax for estates exceeding the

$600,000 exempt amount since there are ways to make gifts without using up your gift/death tax exemption.

If you do make a death-bed gift and you later recover from your "terminal" illness, you should be prepared for hearing the news that your son has already invested (and possibly lost) your life savings in a can't miss deal.

HINT: If you are thinking of making a death-bed gift, have your attorney review with you the death tax, gift tax, income tax and property tax issues of such a gift. Also, see if it makes sense to skip making the gift and, instead, let your children inherit from you through a living trust that avoids probate. Finally, ask how a gift now could save assets for the family if you had a medical catastrophe in the future.

Life insurance is automatically exempt from death tax.

QUESTION: I am a widow. My assets total $600,000. I'm about to buy a life insurance policy that will pay $300,000 upon my death. I'm naming my two children as the beneficiaries on the policy. Since I'm entitled to a $600,000 exemption from death tax, will there be any death tax due? I've heard that there is no death tax on life insurance.

Yes, you are allowed to exempt $600,000 in assets from death tax (with certain exceptions).

But if you own (and/or) control life insurance, it's counted as part of your federal taxable estate for federal death tax purposes.

Since this proposed life insurance will push you over the $600,000 exemption limit, your estate will have landed in the taxing zone, a zone that starts at the 37% rate and goes up from there.

What this means is that with the scenario described by you, there will be a death tax of over $100,000 on the insurance policy proceeds (the 37% tax rate times the $300,000 in life insurance proceeds equals a tax of $111,000).

So, instead of your two children being the sole beneficiaries of the policy, your children would share the proceeds with a certain governmental entity that considers itself to be part of your family, good old Uncle Sam.

There are two ways, however, to keep the insurance proceeds from being taxable for death tax purposes: either have an "irrevocable life insurance trust" (i.e., a trust that cannot be changed) or have your children own, apply for and pay for the policy.

HINT: Ask your attorney whether a life insurance trust or direct ownership by your children makes sense for you. The time to ask about all of this is *before* you apply for a policy although certain steps can be taken to utilize existing policies, too.

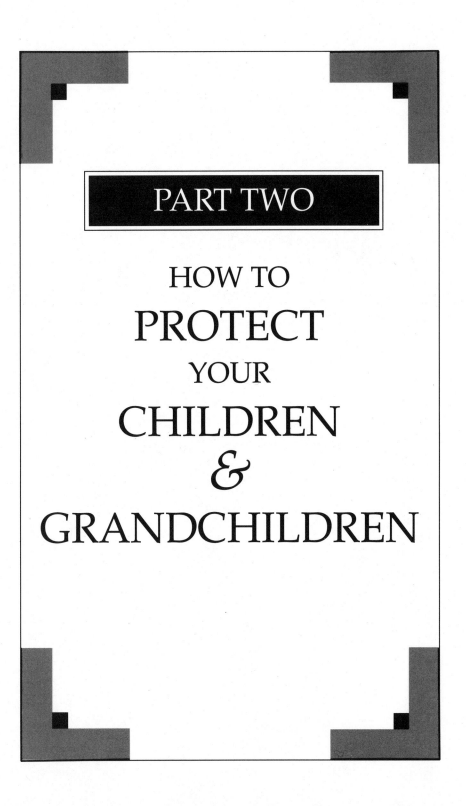

PART TWO

HOW TO
PROTECT
YOUR
CHILDREN
&
GRANDCHILDREN

A Dozen Words and Phrases You Need to Know

QUESTION: When I meet with my attorney, what legal terminology do I really have to know?

There are so many legal terms. Fortunately, you *don't* need to know most of them. By understanding the following words and phrases, however, you'll do just fine. Any other legal words you understand in this area will just be gravy.

1. **Death tax** is a catch-all term for a variety of federal and state taxes that may be due after a death. Yes, Virginia, the government gets to tax you while you are alive and then it gets one last crack at disturbing your final rest. Be assured, however, there are ways to plan in advance to minimize the disturbance.

2. **Gift tax** is a catch-all term for a variety of federal and state taxes that may be due whenever you make a gift during your lifetime.

Now that you're a tax expert, let's move on to wills and trusts.

3. A **will** is a legal document spelling out the distribution of your assets after you die.

4. A **holographic will** is a handwritten will that usually

results in higher lawyer's fees to unscramble and interpret what a person really meant to say.

5. A **testamentary trust** is a trust created under a will. If your will gives assets *directly* to someone with no strings attached, then those assets are *not* left in a trust. You establish a testamentary trust when you leave assets to someone with strings attached. The do's and don'ts of the strings you attach are the provisions of the trust. In a testamentary trust, you spell out who benefits, when and for what purposes. You also say who's in charge of your money. That person or entity is called a trustee. If you name two trustees, they're called co-trustees.

6. An **executor** is the person or entity you name in your will to manage your assets right after you die.

7. A **living trust** is a legal document spelling out the management and distribution of your assets while you are alive *and* after you die (a testamentary trust only operates after you die). The main difference between a will and a living trust is that a living trust may avoid the probate court altogether upon a death.

8. A **trustee** is the person or entity you appoint in your testamentary trust or in your living trust to manage your assets.

9. **Probate** is the court process by which your assets are transferred from you (actually from your estate) to your successors after you die.

10. A **living will** is a "pull-the-plug" document dealing with removal of life support in certain terminal situations.

11. A **durable health power of attorney** is a document by which you appoint an agent to make health care decisions for you.

12. A **durable power of attorney for finances** is a document by which you appoint an agent to manage your money and other assets.

Now, that wasn't so bad.

Why have a will?

QUESTION: My husband and I are both working parents. We have two small children and our lives are very busy. Why should we take time out of our busy busy schedules to have wills prepared for us?

The best way to answer your question is to tell you what will probably happen if the two of you *don't* have wills.

If you die with a will, you are dying "testate." If you die *without* a will, you are dying "intestate."

When you die intestate, your state's laws will write a "will" for you. It's not really a will. It's a set of rules that says one size fits all. Here's how it could be for your spouse, children and other loved ones: just too bad if your family's special circumstances aren't helped or met by the state's will. If you died without a will, it's too late to try to rewrite the state's will.

What kind of a will will your state write? It will depend, of course, on the laws in your state. Keep in mind that the laws as written today may not be the ones in effect at the time you die. By not having signed your own will, you've in essence signed a blank check, without any direction from you, to let your state divvy up your assets and determine who will raise your children.

How are your assets divided up when you don't have a will? It depends. Your assets may go to your spouse, your children, your parents or other heirs. What if the state-mandated division causes a hardship on the one(s) you love and benefits others that you hate? There's nothing you can do about it now that you're gone.

If your state leaves everything to your spouse, then your children may ultimately inherit nothing if your spouse remarries and names spouse number two as the beneficiary.

This unplanned division of assets can have other effects, too. It can result in tens or hundreds of thousands of dollars in extra death taxes, attorney's fees and costs. Your failure to plan your estate could also allow your children to receive huge sums of money in their hands, all in one lump sum, at the tender age of 18.

If a 15-year-old teenager knows, for example, that in three years a tremendous amount of money will be handed to him, he might think, "Why bother with high school? I'm going to be rich!" Even if the teenager stays in high school and studies, how many 18 year olds that are handed a check for a $250,000 life insurance inheritance could resist the impulse to travel and spend, rather than go on to college?

Perhaps the most important reason to have a will is to use it to name a guardian for your children. If you don't have a will, how does the law decide who will be the guardian to raise your children and manage their assets? It's usually based on the closeness of the relative. Are the relatives given preference under the law the ones you'd choose to raise your kids? Are their ethical and religious values ones you share? Are you pleased with how they are raising their own kids (or how they raised you)? In fact, do you want any of your relatives raising your children or would you prefer certain friends to have that responsibility?

There are two kinds of guardians. The guardian who raises your child is the "guardian of the person." The guardian who handles assets owned by your children is the "guardian of the estate." Sometimes one individual serves as both guardian of the person and guardian of the estate. Both kinds of guardians are entitled to a fee from your assets for taking care of your child's welfare and your child's money. This can lead to unqualified relatives and "friends" trying to get this fee-paying job.

HINT: What is more precious than your family? You owe it to them to get your estate planning in order. Keep in mind that if your children's welfare and inheritance is up for grabs, there not only may be fighting within your family but also with your spouse's family. Neither you nor your spouse, the connecting links, may be there to mediate or unite these strangers united by your marriage. If you want to gamble, buy a lottery ticket–but don't die without a will or trust.

Although you may decide not to give anyone a copy of your will or trust in order to keep the provisions private, some relatives or friends should know where the original is kept.

Your will and/or trust should be kept in a safe place where your spouse, executor or trustee can get to it quickly and easily. Possibly your attorney should keep the original. If you are thinking of using a safe deposit box, find out the procedures for opening the box upon your death and who would then be authorized to remove your will and/or trust from the box.

Should I also have a letter of instruction?

QUESTION: I just signed the will prepared by my attorney. Although the will says who gets what when I'm gone, there are a lot of matters that are not covered in the will. Should I have a letter of instruction, too?

It depends. If you do write such a letter, give a copy to your attorney before anyone else sees it to make sure this "non-legal" document does not create a conflict with your will and other estate plan arrangements.

What is in a letter of instruction depends upon your personal circumstances. A typical letter would include information about funeral arrangements, the persons to be notified about your death, the location of your assets and special arrangements regarding your children or other loved ones.

HINT: Take a look at the Appendix in this book for various reference materials.

Keeping your will current

QUESTION: My husband and I signed our wills so long ago I can't remember the decade, let alone the year. We don't know who has our original wills. I know our kids were small when our wills were signed and we had less than $5,000 in assets. Our kids are now in their twenties and our net worth is over $600,000. We may be moving to another state to retire. We are getting nervous about the status of our wills. Should we do something?

Yes. You bring up several important points.

First, keep your will current. To carry out your wishes, a will has to continue to reflect your personal and financial situation.

A will should be reviewed with your attorney whenever a) you marry or divorce or b) there's a marriage, birth, death or divorce of any beneficiary, potential beneficiary, executor or trustee.

Changes in your financial situation may also lead you to revise your will. As your net worth increases, you may want to take advantage of tax planning techniques to minimize or eliminate death tax. With certain exceptions, it's too late to do death tax planning after a death.

HINT: Once you've decided to make a change, you need to decide whether the change should be accomplished by amending your existing document or by creating a whole new document.

Let's say you decide to delete a beneficiary or executor from your will. If you do this through an amendment, the former beneficiary or executor would receive a notice from the probate court after you died. The reason for this is that, in general, everyone named in wills and amendments to wills receives a notice after a death.

Since wills need to be "admitted" (i.e., approved) by the probate court to go into effect, the deleted beneficiary or deleted executor could challenge the amendment (and the deletion) to block approval of the amendment. This could lead to an expensive fight.

Perhaps a better way to go is to have a whole new will prepared that does not even mention the deleted beneficiary or executor.

There's another time when you should consider having a whole new will or trust rather than an amendment. If you have too many amendments, it may be too difficult to understand your documents. If your attorney has kept your existing will or trust on a computer disk, there may even be less legal expense in having a new will prepared as compared to making an amendment to an amendment.

Here's another reason to update your will. Just as your life changes, so do the federal and state laws and regulations. In order to receive tax benefits, your will or trust must reflect those new laws and regulations. The IRS does not knock on your door or send you a letter saying you better update your will or trust. That's why you need to review your will or trust with an estate planning attorney from time to time (ideally, once a year).

Just because your will or trust qualified for certain tax benefits when you signed it does not mean that it will also qualify under changes in the law that occur after you signed the document.

When your will or trust needs to be updated, for whatever reason, you should not make the changes, additions or revisions yourself. You may cause the entire document to be invalid and thrown out. Instead, have your attorney prepare an amendment or a new document, as the case may be.

Finally, when you move or acquire real estate in another state you should have an attorney in that other state review your will or trust to be sure the requirements of that state are satisfied, too.

Importance of updating your beneficiary designations

QUESTION: I am recently divorced. My ex-husband is still named as the beneficiary on some savings accounts if I die. Also, I have my father as the primary beneficiary on my life insurance and I really want my two kids to get those benefits. I have my mother as the primary beneficiary on my retirement plan and she is deceased. There is no secondary, contingent beneficiary named on the retirement plan. Is it a good idea to keep these things up to date?

Yes. You've raised three different issues. First, you probably don't want to take any chances of your ex-husband benefitting from your death. The law in your state may disallow such inheritances after a divorce, but what if you end up living in another state where the law is different with that same account still open? Why have any controversy at all?

Second, you want the "right" beneficiaries named on your life insurance. You want to name your adult children as the primary beneficiaries on your life insurance. Before you stop there, you need to ask yourself who you'd want to benefit if one child died before you, leaving a surviving child (your grandchild). Would you want your grandchild to benefit from the life insurance, too? Your grandchild might need the insurance proceeds more than your remaining living adult child. Your designation needs to reflect your decision regarding a grandchild.

Third, if you have a gap in your retirement plan designation so that there is no named living beneficiary, the benefits might go through the probate court. That would increase the attorney's fees due from your death. Even if the retirement plan would pay benefits to your children where there's a gap in the beneficiary designation, it would not be easy for your children to prove your mother's death if she died 20 years ago in a location unknown to them (especially if they were very young children at the time of her death). Make it easier, not harder, for your children by keeping your designations up to date.

HINT: After you've signed your will or trust, your responsibility as a parent is not over. Make sure your beneficiary designations and title on assets work with, not against, your estate plan. Review all the details with your attorney before signing anything.

Making sure your kids ultimately inherit your assets

QUESTION: I remarried ten years ago and my wife and I are very happy together. I have three lovely children from my first marriage. My wife does not have much in the way of assets. If something happened to me, she would not be able to live on her own means. Is there any way I can benefit my wife and still be sure that my kids ultimately inherit my assets?

It depends. Your will or living trust can have a trust that says in essence, "Take care of my surviving spouse while she is alive, but make sure what is left over goes where I say." This kind of trust allows you to control the ultimate destination of the assets remaining after you and your spouse are gone. However, if your spouse needs all of the assets to live on, there may nothing left to go to your children.

This kind of trust is used very often when there is a second marriage and children by an earlier marriage.

More and more, it's being used in first marriages, too, as a way to protect the children's inheritance.

One alternative is to leave everything or certain assets outright to the surviving spouse. If you do this, you will lose control over what your surviving spouse will do with assets inherited from you. Even if you trust your spouse completely, might she be talked into something that's unwise?

Another alternative is to leave some assets directly to your children upon your death and have other assets in trust for your wife. The question you'll have to answer is whether your wife will have enough to meet her living expenses with this kind of arrangement.

HINT: Surviving spouses sometimes have certain rights, notwithstanding what you put in your will or trust. Ask your attorney what portion of your estate your spouse might receive even if your spouse is written out of your will.

Make sure you update your beneficiary designations, too. Ask what rights your spouse may have as to your retirement plans and IRAs. Your spouse may be getting the balance of your retirement plan after your death with nothing passing on to your children unless your spouse signs a special kind of waiver of his or her rights.

Double-check with your attorney as to how you hold title to (i.e., own) assets. Find out whether you need to change title so that your estate plan is not turned upside down by having the title override the plan in your will or trust.

Finally, to protect your children, talk to your attorney about the wisdom of having a financial agreement with your spouse.

41

Distribution in one lump sum or over time to my kids

QUESTION: I am divorced and I have two adult children. They're 21 and 23. Neither one has ever had or handled much money. They each inherited about $50,000 from their father a year ago and they've spent it already on having a good time. Should I be concerned about leaving all of my estate (I'm worth about $600,000, including life insurance and retirement plans) outright to my kids?

Yes. Although one approach is to say that whatever they do with your money after you're gone is not your concern, that's not really true. You'll always be their mother, even after you're gone. And, as a parent, you want to do the right thing for your children.

In a sense, you're lucky. You've seen what your children did with the inheritances from your ex-husband. You should learn from that experience so it is not repeated.

First, you should have a talk with your children about how they handle money. Their responses might give you fresh insight as to their thinking process and guide you towards the right approach for each of them. And, remember, you might come up with a different approach or solution for each of them. Your children did not come out of a cookie cutter as identical human beings, so the best planning for each of them might be different.

Next, you'll probably want to talk to your attorney about establishing a trust for each child. A trust can be written to be very generous or very restrictive (or something in between) in providing for your children as long as the trust remains in effect.

What you may want to consider is to have the trust automatically end in stages such as one third to be distributed to them starting at age 25 (or later), another third at age 30 and the balance at age 35. This way your children would have three chances at blowing the money. Hopefully, they'll have learned by the time the third, and last, opportunity comes up.

HINT: It's always hard to say what the right ages are for the automatic distribution of assets to your children.

There are several factors to consider in designing the plan for your children. Besides their ages, think about their levels of schooling, their abilities, income, current net worth and future prospects.

If circumstances permit, you might make a considerable gift to your children during your lifetime to obtain additional insight as to how they might handle larger sums after you're gone.

In general, if your children are not very responsible or there are other factors calling for assets left to them to stay in trust, you should space out distributions in two to three automatic payments, each one three to five years apart.

If you have very young children where it's impossible to say how they'll handle money, you'll probably want to hedge your bets and start automatic distributions no earlier than age 25, with additional distributions at 30 and/or 35. The reason for picking age 25 is the hope that your children will have completed their schooling before coming into your money (unless the money is needed for their schooling).

You also need to indicate in the trust how non-automatic distributions are to be made until the trust is terminated. You should think about having generous distributions for such things as the health, support, maintenance and education of your children.

Another possible approach is to have the trust end in stages keyed to a certain number of years after you're gone, such as one third five years after your death, another third ten years after your death and the balance fifteen years after your death.

If you use this approach, you might also want to plug in ages for distribution, too, so that the first distributions occurs five years after you are gone or when a child attains age 30, whichever occurs first. Otherwise, if your children are at least age 40 when you pass away, they might have to wait until age 55 (15 years after your death) or later to receive the balance of their trust. Come to think of it, that may be exactly what you have in mind.

Finally, ask yourself whether you are doing your kids a favor by treating them all the same. They are different people. Should your estate plan reflect those different needs and personalities? While you really can't parent from the grave, you can provide incentives and direction. But be realistic, however, and don't put the trustee in a bind, especially if the trustee is one of your children trying to manage money for another of your children.

How to build flexibility into your plan

QUESTION: We have four children and they each have different needs. Two of them are in grammar school. The third one is a teenager who has just started his college education and the oldest one is only age 23, but she's very well off financially. We're not sure we want to divide everything up into four equal shares. Do you have any ideas?

Yes. There are a couple of questions you should ask yourselves. First, is there a compelling reason (e.g., fairness) why you should divide up the assets equally? Second, should you combine any shares together so that there will be more money on hand to meet a special need of any one of your children?

Perhaps you should have two different division plans, one if any of your children are under age 21 and another if they are all over age 21. You might give more to younger children under the age of 21 who have not had the opportunity to complete their college education, or to a child who obviously has a greater need than the others.

HINT: Instead of creating four shares (whether equal or unequal) to be held in trust for your children, you might consider creating a "family pot trust." A family pot trust holds the shares of two or more children in one trust and allows them to benefit as

46

needed (often unequally) from the assets in the trust.

The reason to consider this approach is to be able to help a child that may have a greater need than the others. If you were alive and would give more to the child in greater need, why not have your trust be able to do the same? The potential disadvantage of this approach is that one child may get the benefit of most or all of your assets to the exclusion of the others.

One way around this disadvantage is to mix and match. You can create separate trusts for the children with some of the assets as well as a family pot trust with the remaining assets.

For example, you might want to allocate 80 percent of your assets in 4 equal shares of 20 percent each. The remaining 20 percent could be kept in a family pot trust that would have flexibility to provide more for some of the children than others. At a certain point, say when all of your then living children were at least age 21, the family pot trust could end and then be divided equally among your then living bloodline.

Another way of providing flexibility is to spell out the permitted uses of your assets for your children and make them as broad as possible. Think about how hard it is to predict all the circumstances your children will face as long as the trust exists.

If you are very restrictive and you say that money may only be spent for education, will a medical operation that exceeds a child's insurance limits be paid from your assets? Instead of drawing the pursestrings too tightly, consider giving your trustee broad discretion to provide for your kids from your assets.

You better count all the heads, carefully.

QUESTION: I have three children. I am disgusted with my son. So, when I had my will prepared, I only told my attorney about my two daughters and the will only benefits them. As far as I'm concerned, my son is dead.

As far as the law is concerned, your son may be alive. If you do not alert your attorney to all of your children, step-children and foster children, your loved ones could be in for a big surprise when your assets are divided up in a way you did not intend.

HINT: Be sure to account for everyone when you meet with your attorney. Why invite your son to contest your will? Find out what steps you can take to minimize or eliminate shares for those of your bloodline you feel are not deserving to profit from your labors. Also, ask whether by excluding a child you are also excluding the bloodline of that child. You may or may not want to do this, too.

Protecting your grandchildren if a child dies before you

QUESTION: I am a widow. I have three children. Two of my children have their own children. My only assets are my house worth $200,000 and a retirement plan with about $100,000 in it. My will leaves everything equally to my surviving children. My beneficiary designation on the retirement plan reads the same way. If a child of mine passes away before me, are my grandchildren (the children of my deceased child) protected the way things are now?

Probably not. It sounds like only your children who survive you will benefit under your will or under the retirement plan. So, if all three of your children survive you, it's divided up three ways. If two of your children survive you, it's divided up two ways; and if only one of them survives you, that one child would receive it all. To get a definite answer, the exact wording of your will and the beneficiary designation need to be reviewed.

HINT: If your intent is to benefit grandchildren where a child has died, you might want to name your surviving bloodline (or issue) instead of your surviving children as the beneficiaries. You should review this issue with your attorney to see how things would work out in your state.

Because property tax laws may favor real estate

left to children (but not to grandchildren), you might adopt one approach for your house and another as to your life insurance benefits.

Whatever you do, you'll want to coordinate your beneficiary designation and your will or trust.

Another factor to keep in mind is that the inheritance of the house in itself should not result in income tax (a later sale of the house might result in income tax). However, the receipt of the retirement plan proceeds by the beneficiaries will probably cause income tax to be due. You should remember this when you are designing your overall plan.

Survival periods and who inherits

QUESTION: I am the widow who just asked you about my will and retirement plan. What happens if I name all of my children as beneficiaries and one of them passes away shortly after I do? Will I have lost control over where he leaves my assets?

Yes. You might want your attorney to add a survival period, of say, 30 days, to your will or trust or to your beneficiary designations. That way, if any of your children fails to survive you for at least 30 days, your deceased child would not inherit from you and *your* alternate choice would inherit instead.

HINT: Have your attorney coordinate a survival period for life insurance and other benefits, too.

Let's just look at life insurance. What happens if your children are named as the beneficiaries of a life insurance policy and they all survive you but one of them survives you for just a short period of time, such as ten days?

First, the life insurance proceeds that would be due to the now deceased child might have to go through a probate of the child's estate, thereby increasing the legal fees.

Second, the life insurance proceeds would also be counted as part of your deceased child's estate and might cause or increase death taxes due from your child's estate. There may be ways to correct this through a technique called "disclaiming" (pushing away) where assets are refused and pass on to the next designated beneficiary.

Third, you would lose control over who will inherit the proceeds from your child's estate.

You should know that there are certain times, for tax reasons, when you would want your children to inherit from you even if they only survive you for a short period of time. There is a special kind of death tax (called a "generation-skipping transfer tax") that may be imposed on inheritances by *grandchildren*, but not on inheritances by children. In general, this generation-skipping transfer tax applies only to larger estates.

You should review with your attorney the advantages and disadvantages of having a survival period and what the survival period, if any, should be in your estate plan.

Protecting gifts and inheritances if your children get divorced

QUESTION: I've made some gifts to my children. My children are both married. Some of the gifts were made before they got married and some of them were made during their marriages. I do not know what they have done with the gifts. They may have commingled (shared) the gifts with their spouses. Both of their marriages are rocky and now I'm concerned about what would happen to these gifts or any inheritance if my children divorced. Could my son-in-law and daughter-in-law end up with any portion of these assets instead of my grandchildren?

Maybe. This is an area of law that's changing quite a bit. You need to talk to your attorney about several matters.

First, let your attorney advise you on how the laws read in the states where your children live now (and in the state where they might be moving) for inheritances as well as for gifts made before and during a marriage.

Second, ask your attorney what legal advice your children should get now on how to hold title to the assets that have been and will be received from you.

HINT: Also, ask your attorney whether a trust would be the best way to handle any inheritance from you. With a trust, the ultimate beneficiaries (your grandchildren) might be better protected and your children could still receive benefits during their lifetime, too.

Making sure you account for lifetime gifts

QUESTION: My will calls for certain gifts to my brothers and sisters off the top with the balance going to my children. For tax reasons (and just to see the happy looks on the faces of my brothers and sisters), I've already given my siblings their gifts while I'm alive. Should I bother changing the provisions in my will that benefit them or will these lifetime gifts automatically take care of any confusion?

Why have any confusion? Why not update your will to reflect that your brothers and sisters have already been taken care of completely? To leave matters as they are may cause hard feelings within the family if someone thinks they are not getting their full share.

HINT: In general, if you have a nagging doubt about a situation, you should clarify it now so unnecessary fights can be avoided. When the connecting link (you) is gone, it is too easy for relatives to feel unrelated when it comes to a fight for money.

How to help prevent lawsuits and will contests

QUESTION: We have four children and one of them is a problem child. As far as we're concerned, the problem child deserves nothing from us and he will receive nothing from our estates. We disinherited the problem child in our wills so there won't be any fights over our assets when we're both gone. Any other thoughts?

Maybe you should think about taking out "will-contest insurance." I'm only half-kidding. Since your problem child will receive nothing under your wills but might get one fourth if the wills are thrown out, what's to discourage him from contesting (challenging) your wills?

Instead of leaving him out entirely, what if you left him "just enough" with the condition that anyone challenging your wills gets nothing? You might have purchased very cheap "will-contest insurance."

HINT: Don't let your emotions lead you down a path that will actually defeat your goals. Sometimes giving a little may buy a lot of peace of mind for the whole family.

Here are a few other ideas to avoid or minimize fights and lawsuits.

First, think ahead as to who would want personal items such as jewelry, furniture and the cars. Do you want to limit the potential takers of these more personal items to just your *children* as compared to *children and grandchildren?*

Remember, if grandchildren are also beneficiaries of these personal items, they may be represented by their surviving parent (your son-in-law or daughter-in-law). It may be more difficult for your surviving children to negotiate with your son-in-law or daughter-in-law.

Second, if your children cannot agree on a division of assets such as furniture and jewelry, you might want to spell out in your will the procedure for resolving any dispute. You could have the executor or trustee divide up the assets into shares and assign them to the children. If you name any child as the executor or trustee, watch out for a conflict of interest in dividing up the shares.

You could also let your children cut a deck of cards and start dividing up assets based upon the cards drawn. The child who drew the highest card could pick the very first item and the other three children would make their initial choices, with the one drawing the second highest card picking second and so on. After the first round of picks, the order would be reversed so that the one drawing the lowest card would select first. Then, the next round would resume with the one who initially drew the highest card picking first again and so on.

Third, be clear in your intentions. For example, if you name someone as a beneficiary, you'll want to also say what happens if the beneficiary does not survive you. You should name the alternate taker of the asset. If furniture needs to be shipped to a beneficiary, you should spell out whether the beneficiary is expected to pay the shipping costs.

Fourth, spell out who pays the death tax, if any, on the items received. Unless you say otherwise, a beneficiary receiving jewelry, for example, would be expected to pay the death tax due on the value of the jewelry. Someone has to pay death tax when it's due. You should spell out who will be paying.

Fifth, anticipate objections from anyone who is "hurt" by a provision in your will or trust who might claim you did not anticipate the actual result (e.g., all antiques to my son and the balance of my furniture to my daughter—what's an antique and who will determine that?)

Sixth, as to the main assets in your estate, are you limiting beneficiaries to your living children only or are you also including living children of a deceased child of yours (your grandchildren)? Also, do you want to make any provision for a son-in-law or daughter-in-law when a child does not survive you?

Seventh, to avoid conflicts, you should coordinate the provisions of your will and/or trust with how you hold title to your assets and how you complete your beneficiary designations.

Eighth, visualize how assets will be "shared" by your children and other loved ones who are beneficiaries of your estate. How easy and friendly will be it be for your children to co-own your assets together after you're gone?

Do you have a family business in which only one child is active but you are leaving the business to several children? Does this make sense or are you causing a family fight? Should you instead leave the business just to the one child who works in the business and leave other assets of comparable value to the other children? Do you need to buy additional life insurance to have enough assets of comparable value to leave to the other children?

Finally, when you're disinheriting someone, are you also intending to disinherit the bloodline of that person? So, whether or not your problem child survives you, think about whether you want the children (your grandchildren) of the problem child to share in your estate.

Selecting a personal guardian for your minor children

QUESTION: My husband and I have not gotten around to signing wills since we do not have too much in the way of assets. I keep feeling concerned that we should take care of naming a guardian to raise our children. I know my sister and my husband's brother would want to come in and fight to take the kids but neither of them is the right choice. What should we do?

Talk to your attorney about naming a personal guardian for your minor children. This "guardian of the person" will be the one in charge of raising your children. The guardian of the person makes the decisions about your children's education, religious training (or lack of training) and other matters that you would handle as a parent. This is not a job about managing money for your minor children. You are entrusting someone to instill values in your children and ensure their well-being.

HINT: When you provide your choices to your attorney, list as many qualified people as possible since you do not know who will be willing and able to serve when the time arises. Before your will is completed, you should ask your desired guardians if they'll serve on your behalf and whether they have any special conditions or requests.

One way to evaluate a potential guardian is to take a good look at how they're raising their own children.

Depending upon the age and maturity of your children (and their ability to discuss the subject of your deaths), you might ask them their opinion about the choices you have in mind.

A trickier issue is how you select relatives from each side of your family and in what order. The overriding factor should be the best interests of your children, not whether someone's feelings will be hurt if they are way down or even off your list of potential guardians.

If you know that your guardian will have to move to a larger place or remodel to accommodate your children as part of the family, you should think about providing approval of such expenditures in your will or trust.

Selecting a guardian of your assets (and executor and trustee) for your minor children

QUESTION: My wife and I have two small kids. Do we need to name a guardian for the money we'll be leaving them if we have already named an executor and a trustee in our wills?

Probably yes. If any assets pass from you or from anyone else *directly* to your minor children, someone needs to manage the assets until the children become adults. That someone is called a "guardian of the estate." An example of how assets could pass directly to your children would be if you named your young children as the beneficiaries on your life insurance policy.

Who should be the guardian of the estate? Usually it's the same person you've named as executor or trustee. The guardian of the estate performs a similar job of managing your children's assets.

Who's the right choice for these money-managing jobs? Above all, you want someone who's honest and who has good common sense. A guardian of the estate or executor or trustee does not need to be a financial whiz. However, your representative should be a prudent person who knows when to ask for financial, tax or legal advice and does so.

Another factor to keep in mind is whether your choice has any conflict of interest. Will the trustee inherit assets that are not paid out to other beneficiaries? Is the trustee your business partner who might be swayed by considerations that affect the partner's interest in the business? Some people are saints and you can trust them completely.

HINT: Try to avoid having assets pass directly to minor children and ending up in a "guardianship." Here's why.

A guardianship involves a separate court proceeding with attorneys fees and court costs.

A guardianship ends when a child becomes an adult. This could mean that each of your children would receive a lump sum payment of $250,000 in life insurance proceeds on their eighteenth birthday. This might mean the end of a college education and the beginning of an around-the-world spending spree.

If, instead, assets were left in trusts for your children, a more orderly and lengthy distribution process could be implemented.

Work with your attorney in coordinating what will happen to all of your assets.

How to have someone watch over your guardian

QUESTION: How can I be sure the guardian I've selected is really going to take care of my kids?

One common way is to name one person as a guardian of the person (the one raising your children) and a different person as the guardian of the estate (the one managing your children's money). That way, the one holding your assets could have some financial control over what was done by the one raising your children and vice versa.

HINT: One additional way to get some peace of mind would be for you to also appoint an advocate in your will or trust.

An advocate would be a sort of guardian angel who would make sure the guardians, executor and trustee were treating your children properly and looking out for their best interests.

Your will or trust document could say that your assets would pay for any legal expenses incurred by the advocate if the advocate felt a court action had to be brought to protect your children (whether the advocate won or lost).

When you pick an advocate (or any representative

of your estate or trust), consider whether there could be any conflict of interest. For example, do the remaining assets in your child's trust go to the advocate when your child dies? Perhaps, the advocate may be guided by ulterior motives and won't be as aggressive for your children if that's the case.

You might select a guardian from one side of your family and an advocate from the other side as a way of keeping everyone involved and on their best behavior.

You should also name backup advocates in case your first or second choice is unable to serve.

Should you have a bank or trust company as your executor or trustee?

QUESTION: We have four children. They do not get along with one another. None of them knows how to manage money. In fact, we're not too good at it either. Our estate plan will require certain tax decisions and steps to be taken at the time the first of us passes away. When we're both gone, we have set up trusts for the children that will allow the trustee to decide how much should be paid out to the children. Should we name a bank or trust company as the executor and trustee in our wills?

Probably yes. After a death, your estates are entitled to certain tax benefits if your executor or trustee completes all the necessary steps on time. A professional executor or trustee such a bank or trust company might be the right choice when one of you is gone.

When you are both gone, it sounds like none of your children have a sufficient understanding of financial matters to serve as a trustee. Even if they did, you need to determine whether it would be a burden for one child to decide how much to distribute to another child. Also, there might be a conflict of interest if whatever wasn't distributed by a trustee/child to a non-trustee/child might ultimately be inherited by the trustee/child.

HINT: You might consider a co-trustee arrangement whereby the surviving spouse would serve together with a professional trustee.

Or, if you did have confidence that the surviving spouse could serve alone as the trustee, you might give the spouse the power to name a co-trustee to help out if needed.

You need to work with your attorney on this issue so that other relevant factors such as the size of your estates and the composition of your assets is considered.

Some professional trustees only take on estates of a certain size or charge a minimum fee that might be too high for a smaller estate. Also, you might want some assets retained for the long run, whereas a professional trustee might feel uncomfortable keeping those assets (such as an active business) for liability reasons.

How can I be sure my executor or trustee won't run away with my money?

QUESTION: If my husband and I are gone, we want to name my cousins as our first and second choices as executor. Is there any way to guarantee that one of them won't run away with our money and leave our little children penniless?

Although you can't prevent anyone from running away with your money, to insure against that risk your will or trust can require that after you're gone your cousins take out an insurance policy, known as a bond, with a bonding company.

If your executor or trustee runs away with your money, the bonding company makes good on it for your children and then the bonding company tracks down the wrongdoer. Bonds do cost money, however, and they are a yearly expense that would be paid out of your funds once a cousin is in charge of your assets.

Ask your attorney what a bond would cost your estate and whether there are ways to lower the expense, perhaps by requiring court approval for certain actions.

Many wills and trusts routinely waive the requirement of a bond. It's worth thinking about whether a bond is needed in your case.

HINT: A cheaper form of insurance *might* be to name two people to serve at all times as co-executors or co-trustees (or co-guardians of your children's estate) so that you would reduce the risk that any one person would control and manipulate your funds. However, in some states, naming more than one executor, trustee or guardian may increase the total fee to be paid to these representatives. You may need to balance the cost of a bond as compared to the cost of extra executor or trustee fees.

Remember, if you have doubt about an individual's honesty, that person is probably not a good choice as your representative.

Can it be a financial burden to serve as an executor or trustee?

QUESTION: I own a gas station and the land it's sitting on. There's been some problem with leaking gas tanks but otherwise everything is okay here. I asked my best friend if he would be the executor of my will and he said no. He said that he did not want the liability of running a business or anything to do with leaking gas tanks. Is he paranoid or justified in his concerns?

Probably justified. These days, being an executor or trustee, is not without its risks. Beneficiaries might complain how assets were invested, whether they were sold too soon or too late and how the business was being run. In addition, with the way the law is expanding, it's possible that your executor or trustee could have personal liability for the environmental cleanup of your land. This sounds strange but it's possible. Finally, courts do not always allow a fee to an executor or trustee for all of the work involved in being your representative.

HINT: Talk to your attorney about what the "job" of executor and trustee entails so that you pick the right person or entity for the job. There may be circumstances in your case that would lead you to select a different executor or trustee.

Do you owe your children an inheritance?

QUESTION: I'm having trouble making ends meet. I've helped all my kids through college. I'm now faced with making some difficult choices. Should I take a retirement option that will maximize income for me while I'm alive but leave nothing to my kids or should I get by on less so that they'll inherit something?

Parents are beginning to question how much they "owe" their children. Is it a right or a privilege to have enough left over when you're gone to provide for adult children who've completed their education? More and more, parents are coming to the conclusion that they should not sacrifice in their later years, especially if their children are grown, have completed their education and do not suffer from any disabilities.

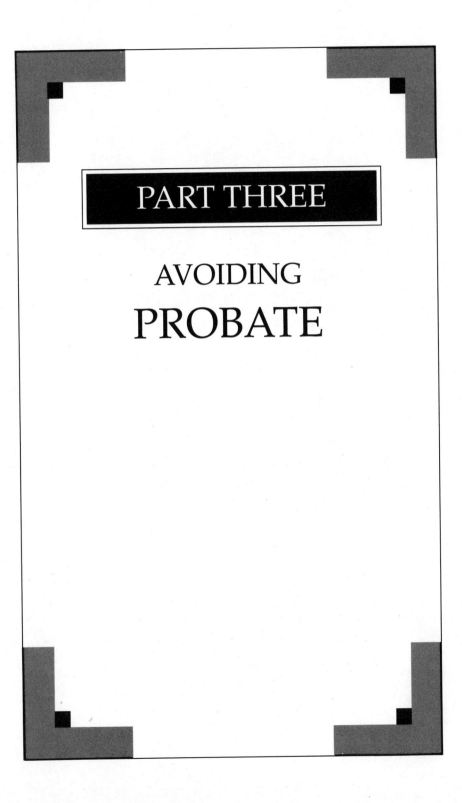

PART THREE

AVOIDING
PROBATE

What is probate?

QUESTION: Everyone tells me I should avoid probate. What is probate?

Probate is the court process by which your assets are transferred from you (actually from your estate) to your successors after you die. The bad news with probate is that the attorney's and executor's fees are usually quite costly (often 2 to 5 percent for the attorney and a similar amount for your executor) and it can take considerable time (usually a year or so) to complete the transfer of your assets to your successors.

Probate takes place after your death. During the process, your assets are located and valued, your creditors and death taxes are paid and, at the end, distribution is made to your successors.

HINT: If you don't have a will, your estate may have to go through probate. If you do have a will, your estate may also have to go through probate. And, if you have a *living trust*, your estate may still have to go through probate.

            The following four factors need to be considered in determining whether an estate must go through probate: 1) how title (ownership) is held, 2) who

is listed as the beneficiary on your assets that
have a beneficiary designation and whether the
named beneficiary survives you, 3) the size (value)
of your estate (certain small estates may escape
probate) and 4) whether you signed a will or a
living trust.

You should discuss these four factors with your
attorney to determine whether your estate will or
should go through probate. It's possible that by
going through probate you may benefit by short-
ening the time period for creditors to make claims
against your estate. In your state, creditors may
have more time to go after your assets if you do
not have a probate.

Avoiding probate with a living trust

QUESTION: My wife and I have three grown children. Very briefly, tell me what a living trust is and if we can avoid probate just by signing a living trust?

A living trust is a legal document spelling out the management and distribution of your assets while you are alive *and* after you die. Once you pass away, a living trust is like a will in that it says who gets what and when.

With a living trust, the fees for the attorney are usually much lower after a death as compared to the fees for the attorney handling the probate of a will. Also, in many cases, assets may be transferred to your successors sooner after a death with a living trust than with a will.

Before a living trust can be used to avoid probate, three steps are required. The first step, of course, is signing the trust to put it into effect. That in itself, however, is usually *not* enough to avoid probate.

The second step is transferring the title (ownership) of your assets to the trustee (the manager) of the living trust. In some states you can be your own trustee. In other states, you need to name someone else or a bank or trust company as the trustee while you are alive.

The third step, in some cases, is to complete new beneficiary designations on certain life insurance, retirement
plans and IRAs naming the trustee of the living trust as the
primary or secondary beneficiary, where appropriate.

If you only complete step one, then a probate may be
required when you pass away *even though you've signed a
living trust document.*

HINT: Now you might ask yourself why bother to do step
         one without step two? Well, in some states, you
         cannot act as your own trustee. If that's the case,
         then you'd need to have someone else act as
         trustee while you're alive and that might cost you
         a trustee's fee every year. Also, you might not be
         comfortable having someone else acting as the
         trustee for you.

         Know, too, that after your death there are death
         tax and income tax implications relating to the
         transfer of title of assets to your living trust and
         the naming of beneficiaries on beneficiary
         designations. Ask your attorney what's most
         beneficial in your case.

         A living trust is not for everyone. You need to
         review your situation with your attorney to see
         whether a living trust is right for you.

The advantages and disadvantages of a living trust

QUESTION: What's so good about a living trust?

A living trust can reduce the fees and costs after your death by a considerable amount.

A living trust can also provide more privacy to your family and loved ones. With a probate of your will, your will and all of your assets that are covered by your will become a public record. This may not be too appealing to you. A living trust is a more private arrangement.

Another possible benefit of a living trust is that you may avoid a court proceeding to determine who'll manage your assets if you become incapacitated. With a living trust, it's easier to have someone else put in charge of your assets once doctors make a determination that you are incapacitated.

If you do *not* have a living trust and you are incapacitated, a court supervised hearing would take place where a judge would determine whether you need a "conservator" (someone to manage your financial affairs). The disadvantage of a such court proceeding is that it could cost you substantial attorney's fees. The advantage, however, is that a judge is looking out for you and your interests.

So, having a living trust that avoids a court conservatorship hearing may not always be beneficial, although it generally is for most people.

HINT: Usually the older and wealthier you are, the more your family can benefit from a living trust. If you own real estate in several states, the trust may allow your successors to avoid a probate in each of those states.

Although joint tenancy and a living trust can each avoid a probate upon your death, assets owned with your children as joint tenants can be exposed to your children's creditors while you are alive. Assets owned by you alone in your living trust should be protected against your children's creditors while you are alive.

Despite its many advantages, there are disadvantages to a living trust, however, as noted below.

The upfront attorney's fees are generally higher for a living trust as compared to a will because, by its very nature, the living trust is a more complex document that usually requires additional time and effort. Also, there is extra work in transferring assets to the living trust after it's been signed that is not present with a will. Ask your attorney what the difference in the attorney's fee would be for having a living trust as compared to a will.

In general, you can do the same death tax planning with a will as with a living trust. And, in some cases, you can do more intricate after-death income tax planning with a will going through probate than with a living trust.

If you refinance a property, there may be some extra work and expense in connection with the loan if your property is held in a living trust.

A probate of a will after your death may afford your estate greater protection against creditors than would a living trust. In your state, creditors may have more time to go after your assets if you do *not* have a probate.

When you have a living trust, you need to have a special accompanying will known as a "pourover will." Its purpose is to ensure that any assets you may not have transferred to your living trust while you were alive are "poured over" into your living trust. These poured over assets will go through probate so it's a good idea to review with your attorney which assets you are not transferring to your living trust and the reasons you are not making the transfer. In some cases, you might keep assets outside of your living trust and use a pourover will if your state requires someone else to be the trustee of your living trust during your lifetime.

Why is title so important?

QUESTION: My wife and I recently signed wills. Does it really matter to us or our kids how my wife and I hold title to our assets?

Yes. How you hold title can determine 1) whether your will or trust can say who inherits your assets, 2) when your successors will receive your assets, 3) whether the assets will have to go through probate to get to your successors, 4) how much death tax will be paid by your family, and 5) how much income tax the surviving spouse will pay in the future.

Everyone thinks a will or trust must control who will receive your assets after you're gone. The truth is that a will or trust *may* or *may not* control who gets what after a death, depending upon how you held title to your assets. If you do not hold title to your assets in a way that's best for your particular circumstances, your will or trust might have as little to say about who inherits from you as does your grocery list.

The reason for this is that there are many different ways to hold title and each way has a different result in different circumstances. You are free to choose how you hold title, but you must understand that this choice can have tremendous consequences in the future.

Title says who owns it, how much of it and in what way. There are many ways to hold title including joint tenancy, tenancy in common, community property, tenants by the entirety, as an individual who's unmarried or single, as a married person, and in a trust. Different states have rules as to the different ways in which you can hold title.

How you hold title can determine whether an asset has to go through the probate court or other court proceeding or whether it may be given directly to a beneficiary right after you die.

Title affects the answers to these five important questions about each of your assets:

1. Who gets it?
2. How soon will it be given?
3. Will it go through probate before being distributed?
4. How expensive will the legal fees be in distributing it to my successors?
5. How much will the government take in taxes?

Now that I have your attention, let's explore title a bit further. Again, title is the way in which you tell the world who owns a particular asset. By way of example, let's look at how holding title as joint tenants affects these five questions. Joint tenancy is a very common way for two or more people to hold title together.

Who gets it?

Upon a death, joint tenancy says to the world "Give this

asset automatically to the person or persons who hold title as joint tenants with me even if my will or trust says differently." In other words, *joint tenancy overrides your will or trust*. So, barring a lawsuit after your death that challenges your understanding of how joint tenancy works, the asset will go to the surviving joint tenant(s) despite your other intentions. For example, if you own a house with a friend in joint tenancy but you really wanted your children to inherit it upon your death, you've picked the wrong way to hold title.

Joint tenancy can be the right way to hold title in some cases. It just depends upon a lot of factors that your attorney needs to review with you.

How soon will it be given?

In general, joint tenancy can be a very quick way to transfer title upon a death. However, in California, for example, a surviving spouse can receive non-joint tenancy assets passing outright to the spouse within just two months of a death. Of course, assets that go through the probate court will take longer to be distributed.

Will it go through probate before being distributed?

Joint tenancy usually avoids probate. Why do I say usually? Let's say a husband and wife own a house in joint tenancy. Although a probate would be avoided when the first spouse died, a probate would be required when the second spouse died if other steps (such as creating a living trust) were not taken before the second spouse's death.

Actually, if the husband and wife died together, say in a car crash or a plane crash, there would be a probate of each of their interests in the house.

How expensive will the legal fees be in distributing it to my survivors?

Joint tenancy is relatively inexpensive to handle upon a death. It may cost much less than one percent of the asset value in legal fees. Probates can be costly, ranging from a few percent to 10 percent or so of the assets probated.

How much will the government take in taxes?

How you hold title can affect the income tax payable by your successors, the death tax and, in some states, the property tax paid after a death. If you do not coordinate how you hold title with the death tax and income tax planning in your will or trust, then the tax planning may be of no effect. Holding title as joint tenants can result in higher taxes.

HINT: You should coordinate your will or trust with how you take title to your assets and how you complete your beneficiary designations. The world is too complex for you to determine this on your own without legal and tax assistance.

Joint tenancy

QUESTION: I don't want to bother with the expense or paperwork involved in setting up a living trust. I've heard that just putting my spouse and my children on title to my assets in joint tenancy will do the job quickly and cheaply. Have I heard wrong?

You've only heard part of the story. Joint tenancy can work out sometimes. Joint tenancy could be renamed joint risk taking. If your children co-own assets with you, then their creditors (and spouses who divorce them, possibly) might get their hands on "your" assets while you are alive. When you put someone on title as a joint tenant, you are announcing to the world, "Here's a new, current co-owner!"

With husbands and wives, there may be income tax disadvantages with joint tenancy if the surviving spouse sells an asset after the first spouse has died. Ask your attorney whether taking title to your assets as community property is possible in your state, and if it is, whether it makes sense to do so.

If your goal is to avoid probate on both of your deaths and also avoid being responsible for your adult children's debts and actions, you should talk to your attorney about setting up a living trust instead of holding title as joint tenants.

HINT: Joint tenancy can have other complications, too. Let's say you put a child on title as a joint tenant on your house and your child later becomes incapacitated when you want to sell the house. To complete the sale, you might need to have a court designate a representative for your child (at some expense) to sign the transfer deed.

Also, joint tenancy may only postpone, not avoid, a probate of an asset. Once there is only one surviving joint tenant left and that survivor dies, unless some exception applies, there will be a probate on that final survivor's death.

Totten trusts-another way to avoid probate

QUESTION: I have two children. My main assets are two savings accounts. My furniture and personal belongings are not worth too much. My kids will divide everything equally when I'm gone. I don't want to bother with a living trust. I'm concerned about the risk of putting my kids on title with me on my savings accounts even though they're adults. Is there an inexpensive way to avoid probate without using a living trust or joint tenancy accounts?

Probably yes. Talk to your attorney about totten trust accounts. This is a way of holding title on certain types of accounts that avoids probate at your death but keeps total control in your hands during your lifetime. This approach, unlike joint tenancy accounts, avoids having to give your kids access to any portion of your money while you're alive. Husbands and wives can use this approach, too, so that a probate of the accounts is avoided on the death of each of them.

HINT: There are a few reasons, however, why you may *not* want to use a totten trust. First, for married couples, this may not produce the best result for death tax planning or control purposes since the surviving spouse will own the entire account.

Second, this way of holding title may only benefit

children who survive you but not the bloodline of a child who dies before you.

Third, you may have other assets that will have to go through probate anyway if you do not take other steps such as having a living trust.

The bottom line is that you need to obtain legal advice for your particular situation to come up with the right approach. It may just be that a totten trust is the right way for you to avoid probate.

Special arrangements between spouses

QUESTION: My wife and I have a net worth of around $200,000, including the equity in our house. The title to all of our assets is held in community property. We have two grown children. We want to keep things simple. If we have a will leaving everything outright to the surviving spouse and then to the kids when we're both gone, will a probate be required at each of our deaths or just on the second death?

It depends. On the first death, your state may allow an alternative to a full probate. You need to discuss this with your attorney. If the surviving spouse keeps all of the assets, then a probate would probably be required on the second death. However, if the surviving spouse were to sell the house and put all of the proceeds in totten trust accounts (see page 88), then a probate could be avoided on the second death.

HINT: These special arrangements for spouses may have certain downsides. This "all to the surviving spouse" approach may not produce the best death tax result in larger estates since the surviving spouse will own 100 percent of the assets, increasing the possibility of a death tax when the survivor dies.

Secondly, the surviving spouse will be able to

leave the assets to anyone, including a new spouse, rather than just to the kids. You pay for simplicity. You need to decide if the cost is too dear.

Coordinate your beneficiary designations with your whole plan

QUESTION: I am a widower. I have two kids, James who's 25 years old and Timmy who's 12. My will leaves everything in separate trusts for my two kids until they're age 35. My estate consists of a retirement plan with about $200,000, life insurance of $300,000 and a checking account with $1,000–nothing else. I've named my estate as the beneficiary on my retirement plan. I've named James and Timmy as the beneficiaries on my life insurance. Will there be a probate on my death?

Probably yes. Since you've named *your estate* as the beneficiary on your retirement plan, you have created assets that must go through the court probate system. This will probably mean attorney's fees of thousands of dollars that may have been avoided if you had instead named the trusts under your will as the beneficiary.

HINT: By naming your estate as the beneficiary, you may also have unnecessarily exposed the retirement plan proceeds to claims and debts through a probate.

Although your life insurance policy proceeds will go directly to the kids since you've named them as beneficiaries, there are a couple of problems with this approach.

First, James will get his half of the insurance proceeds right away and not through the trust you established in your will.

Second, Timmy's share will have to be placed in a court guardianship or equivalent since he is a minor. This means that there will be extra attorney's fees to handle these court proceedings. Finally, Timmy will get his share of the life insurance as soon as he is no longer a minor, at age 18.

You should have your attorney review your beneficiary designations to a) see if they work with, and not against, your estate plan and b) to minimize court-related expenses and attorney's fees.

Avoiding gaps in your beneficiary designations

QUESTION: Our main asset is our IRAs. We have named each other as the primary beneficiary but we left the contingent (secondary) beneficiary blank instead of naming our children (who are all grown up). Is this a good idea?

Probably not. You want to avoid gaps in beneficiary designations because of the way the gaps may be filled. It may be that whenever there is no named living beneficiary, the proceeds must go to your estate. This can result in a probate that could have been avoided by naming your children. A probate can mean attorney's fees of thousands of dollars, delays in distribution and exposure to creditors unnecessarily.

HINT: Work with your attorney in coming up with the correct contingent beneficiary designation in case your primary beneficiary does not survive you.

Consider whether a surviving spouse should be named the primary beneficiary to take advantage of certain income tax laws.

Naming the surviving spouse (instead of a trust for the surviving spouse) could have disadvantages, too. For example, the surviving spouse could leave the remaining proceeds to anyone, not just the kids.

Finally, gaps are sometimes automatically filled in for you by the rules and regulations of your IRA. These rules may call for distributing your IRAs to your surviving children. However, by the same token, these rules to fill gaps might not provide for a grandchild where a child of yours passed away before you.

What doesn't avoid probate?

QUESTION: I've heard so many things about probate and avoiding probate that my head is swimming. What doesn't avoid probate?

Where do I start?

First, if you have a living trust (see page 28 for a definition) but you have not properly transferred all of the assets you can to the living trust, you *may* have a probate on those assets outside the trust.

Second, if you have a living trust but you have a gap in your beneficiary designations on life insurance, retirement plan or IRA benefits, you *may* have a probate on those assets.

Third, if you just have a will without a living trust, then you *may* have a probate on the assets covered by your will.

Fourth, if you have a will that contains a testamentary trust (see page 28 for a definition), then you *may* have a probate on the assets covered by your will.

Fifth, if you don't have a will or living trust, then you *may* have a probate on your assets.

Sixth, even if you give someone a power of attorney over

your assets, you *may* have a probate.

HINT: See pages 75 and 76 to review the four factors
that determine whether a probate may be required on your estate. It is essential that your
estate plan be properly drafted to address all the
nitty-gritty details of title and beneficiary designations.

PART FOUR

TAXES,

TAXES,

TAXES

How many types of taxes are there?

QUESTION: When my husband and I are taking care of our wills or trust, the only tax we're really dealing with is a death tax, right?

No. Your wills and trust and the other related documents may involve the following kinds of taxes:

1. Federal death (estate) tax
2. State inheritance tax
3. Federal generation-skipping transfer tax
4. State generation-skipping transfer tax
5. Federal gift tax
6. State gift tax
7. Federal income tax
8. State income tax
9. Federal excise taxes on retirement plans
10. Property tax
11. Local documentary transfer tax

HINT: Before you make a decision about your will, trust or beneficiary designations, you should ask about the tax consequences of that decision. Although taxes should not dictate your decisions, they may certainly lead you to another approach in some cases.

Federal death tax

QUESTION: I am a widow. I have two grown children. I want to leave everything to my children. When you add up everything, I'm worth $200,000. I have IRAs with about $100,000 in them and life insurance of another $100,000. How much federal death tax will there be at my death?

For most people, the magic number is $600,000 as to whether there will be any *federal* death tax. You should pay attention as to how that $600,000 amount is arrived at. First, you add up all your assets such as real estate, cash, stocks, bonds, cars and personal items. Then, you also add up your IRAs, retirement plans and certain life insurance policies (the ones controlled by you) and all of your other assets. Next, you subtract your debts and liabilities (such as mortgages, car loans and personal loans). If what you are left with is below $600,000, then, in general, there will not be any federal death tax.

If you're married, you'll be doing a different calculation as to what you own as compared to what your spouse owns to see how the numbers come out.

Depending upon how a married couple sets up their will or trust, they *could* each have a $600,000 exempt amount which would make a total $1,200,000 exemption. The exempt amount might be lower if gifts are made by either or both spouses during their lifetimes that exceed certain federally established limits.

Also, if you have guaranteed any obligations of someone else, say for your children, the results of the calculation may be very different. You should make your attorney aware of such guarantees even if you never expect to be called upon to pay anything on the obligations guaranteed by you.

Finally, there may be state inheritance tax and/or federal and state income tax even if there is no federal death tax.

Different assets have different tax consequences. For example, if your son receives all of your life insurance benefits, he will probably be getting them without any income tax due on the proceeds. However, if your daughter receives your IRAs, she'll pay income tax on the benefits. So, you may want to name them as equal beneficiaries on the IRAs and as equal beneficiaries on the life insurance. That way they will each receive one half of each asset and share the income tax obligation equally too. This is to be compared with your current plan that could result in your son netting more than your daughter since she'll pay all the income tax.

HINT: Every year you should make up a list of your assets and liabilities to determine how close you are to the $600,000 level. You might want your attorney to take certain extra tax planning steps for you if you are close to or above that amount.

If you are above the $600,000 level, you might

consider making "lifetime gifts."

You can make certain lifetime gifts of up to $10,000 per calendar year per recipient that do *not* use up any part of your $600,000 exemption.

This can be very important if you are terminally ill and want to reduce death tax. Here's an example of how such lifetime gifts could work. If you were worth $700,000 and you had five children, you could give $10,000 to each of your five children in one calendar year (even as late as December) and identical gifts the next January. That way you could remove $100,000 in gifts ($50,000 in December and $50,000 in January) from your estate and save around $37,000 in death tax.

You do not have to be terminally ill to benefit from making lifetime gifts. The larger your estate, the more you should consider making lifetime gifts. However, you should always make a gift with the expectation that you'll never see it again, even if you need it.

Always check with your attorney *before* making gifts as there are many rules that come into play.

Special deduction for married couples

QUESTION: I understand that I can exempt $600,000 from federal death tax on my death. If I leave my wife more than $600,000, will she have to pay death tax at the time of my death?

Not necessarily. If you pass away first and your estate is larger than $600,000, there are ways to leave more than $600,000 to your spouse with no federal death tax due at your death. The way you do this is to qualify for the federal "marital deduction." To do so, your will or trust must meet certain technical requirements which are beyond the scope of this book.

Keep in mind that if the assets you are leaving to your spouse qualify for this marital deduction, there may only be a delay, or deferral, of death tax until your spouse dies. This deduction can eliminate federal death tax when the first spouse dies but the assets that qualify for the deduction are then counted (or what's left of them) in the survivor's taxable estate. There may or may not be death tax due on the survivor's death on those assets.

HINT: Especially if your will or trust was signed before September 12, 1981 or if your surviving spouse is not a U.S. citizen or permanent resident, you need to have your attorney review your will or trust to take full advantage of the marital deduction.

There is a trust called a "QTIP trust" that allows a surviving spouse to get this marital deduction and helps protect the ultimate inheritance for your children. QTIP stands for qualified terminable interest property. Ask your attorney whether this type of trust should be used for any portion of your estate that exceeds $600,000.

Remember, if your will or trust does not contain certain technical provisions, your spouse will *not* qualify for this special deduction. That could lead to an unnecessary tax being paid by your surviving spouse.

Do death tax and gift tax have anything to do with one another?

QUESTION: Can I give away $600,000 in assets during my lifetime with no gift tax? Or, if I decide to wait and give away $600,000 when I'm gone, is there no death tax?

Federal gift tax and federal death tax share one $600,000 exemption to reduce both types of tax.

Gift tax is a tax paid by you on certain types of gifts you make during your lifetime. You pay federal gift tax if these types of lifetime gifts have exhausted your $600,000 exemption.

Death tax is a tax paid if, at your death, your assets minus liabilities exceed your $600,000 exemption (or what's left of the exemption if you've used up some or all of it by making certain types of lifetime gifts).

To summarize, by making gifts during your lifetime you can either use up your $600,000 exemption in full or partially, leaving the balance available at your death. Or, on the other hand, you can leave it all available at your death to shield against federal death tax.

For example, if you qualified for the full $600,000 exemption and you used up $300,000 of the exemption by making lifetime gifts that were in excess of $10,000 per person per calendar year, you would have $300,000 of the exemption left at your death to apply against the death tax.

If your estate is larger than your remaining exemption, your estate is subject to federal death tax on the amount above the exemption. Federal death tax starts at 37% for amounts above $600,000. See page 203 for a chart showing the death tax on estates of different sizes.

HINT: There are ways to exempt more than just the $600,000 amount by making gifts during your lifetime. Only certain kinds of gifts, however, qualify to stretch the exempt amount. So, you should review any proposed gift with your attorney *before* making the gift to see whether it eats into your $600,000 exemption instead of stretching it.

In general, a gift of no more than $10,000 per calendar year per recipient qualifies to stretch the exempt amount. So, if you are a widower and you have four adult children, you could probably give each of them $10,000 this calendar year and not use up any portion of your $600,000 exempt amount. You can also stretch this amount by paying tuition and/or medical expenses *directly to providers* on behalf of the persons you want to benefit.

Husbands and wives can usually double these $10,000 amounts if certain technical requirements are met.

It is important to understand the consequences of lifetime gifts *before* the gifts are made. Some gifts may not reduce the tax on your estate. With advance planning, you can sometimes restructure a gift so that it produces a tax benefit you would otherwise have lost. Since states have their own rules on these matters, you cannot ignore state law consequences.

The "grandparent's tax"

QUESTION: I'm 80 years old. I've heard that there is a special death tax imposed just on grandparents. Is this so? It sounds illegal and un-American.

There is a second type of federal death/gift tax that is sometimes imposed when your grandchildren or great-grandchildren (or other relatives or non-relatives who are much younger than you) inherit or receive gifts from you.

Here's the thinking behind this tax. The IRS wants to have a chance to impose a death tax on your assets when you die. Then, the government wants to have an opportunity to tax your children when they die (including taxing the assets they received from you).

Now, if you leave or give assets so that your grandchildren, not your children, receive them, the IRS feels it would miss a chance to tax those assets when your children die.

So, if you skip a generation (your children's generation) by giving or leaving your assets to your grandchildren, the IRS wants to make up for that lost opportunity by imposing a "generation-skipping tax" in some cases. The good news is that each person can exempt up to $1,000,000 from this tax (married couples can exempt up to a total of $2,000,000). That is $1,000,000 per giver, not $1,000,000 per recipient.

So, a widow or widower with 5 children would have a $1,000,000 exemption, not a $5,000,000 exemption. The generation-skipping tax starts at the 55% rate for amounts above the $1,000,000 exemption.

Due to the huge size of the exemption from this tax (up to $1,000,000), most people won't be affected by this second kind of death/gift tax.

HINT: Your attorney can draft your will or trust to take full advantage of the $1,000,000 per person exemption. With married couples, the exemption may be $600,000, not $1,000,000, for the first spouse to die unless that spouse has a QTIP trust (see pages 106 and 161) in his or her will or trust.

There are also ways to minimize or avoid the "grandparent's tax" by giving certain benefits and powers to your children even if your grandchildren end up inheriting from you.

Are you really leaving your assets just to your kids or to Uncle Sam, too?

QUESTION: I am a widower with two grown children. I have about $600,000 in assets. I was intending to leave all of my assets equally to my two children. My daughter is very wealthy. Now she tells me that whatever I leave to her will be subject to death tax in her estate. Should I leave everything to my son since my daughter is well off?

Maybe. When you are doing tax planning for your estate, you should also be thinking about your children's death tax situation, too. Here's why.

If your daughter's estate (without your assets) would be subject to death tax when she dies, the IRS would take at least 37 percent of your inheritance to her. For example, if she received one-half of your $600,000 estate, the death tax *her* estate would pay on the inheritance when she died would be at least $100,000.

If that inheritance doubled in value by the time she passed away, then the IRS would get at least $200,000.

What's another way of handling your estate? You might leave your daughter's share to her children instead of her. Then those assets would not be taxed in your daughter's estate when she died.

HINT: You should, however, ask yourself a few other questions before making up your mind. First, what if your daughter suffers a financial reversal right before or right after you're gone? Would you want her automatically excluded from your estate? Or, would you want to hedge your bets and set up a trust in your will by which a trustee would have discretion to benefit your daughter and/or her children in a way that would not be included in her taxable estate?

Or, would you rather give your daughter the option of taking or not taking from your estate? There is a gift-tax-free way for your daughter to decline taking from your estate and have it pass to her children (or your son). This technique is called using a disclaimer and it can be very technical in its implementation.

The main point is not to be too quick in assuming the way things are now is the way they'll always be.

Who really pays death tax?

QUESTION: I am a widow with two grown children. I have two assets, my house that is worth $400,000 and life insurance benefits totalling $400,000. I know that there will be death tax due when I'm gone since I'll be worth more than $600,000. I'm naming my son as the beneficiary on the life insurance. My will says my daughter inherits the rest of my assets. My will says death taxes will be paid from my probate estate without reimbursement from any beneficiary. Will each of my kids inherit the same amount after death taxes are paid?

Probably not the way your estate plan reads now.

Your son will receive the insurance proceeds directly from the insurance company so they will not be part of the probate estate under your will.

It appears that your will is charging your daughter's share (your house) with the death taxes on your house *and* the death taxes on the life insurance.

You can change your will so that they each will pay their own fair share of the death tax. Otherwise, your daughter will end up paying her brother's share of the death tax as well as her own.

HINT: Have your attorney take a look at the allocation

of death taxes under your will and/or trust. This is especially important if the beneficiaries under your will or trust are different than the ones you named in beneficiary designations for life insurance, retirement plans and IRAs.

Will income taxes make an equal division unequal?

QUESTION: My husband and I have two grown children. We have two assets to leave to our children—our house and our IRAs. We think our house will be worth about the same as our IRAs. Since our children do not get along well, we were thinking of leaving the house to our daughter and the IRAs to our son. This would avoid co-ownership of the assets between them and avoid fights. Is this a good idea?

Maybe. There are a couple of things to consider.

First, you should be aware of the different income tax consequences to your children. When your daughter inherits your house, it will *not* be income to her. When your son receives your IRAs, it *will* be income to him.

Second, you need to be sure that your will or trust does not result in one child paying all of the other child's share of the death tax.

Third, if the values of the house and the IRA differ at the time you're both gone, one child may end up with far more than the other one.

HINT: Although it may be desirable to avoid co-ownership of assets between certain children, you need to have your attorney review with you the federal and state death tax, income tax and property tax consequences of such a plan. You may want your will or trust worded in such a manner to handle value changes over time.

Retirement plans can be taxed more than you think

QUESTION: My wife and I are very fortunate. We have healthy children and grandchildren. Our house is fully paid for and we have a very large retirement fund that will eventually pass on to our children and grandchildren. Could we ask for anything more?

Yes–different tax laws. Retirement plans have had an interesting tax history. At one point, they were exempt from federal death tax. Then, up to $100,000 was exempt from federal death tax. Now, they are potentially subject to several federal death taxes.

Depending upon a) the size of your retirement fund, b) the value of your other assets and c) the provisions in your will or trust, your retirement fund could be subject to the regular federal death tax, the generation-skipping tax (a second type of federal death tax), state inheritance tax, federal and state income tax and federal excise taxes.

The bottom line is that these taxes might eat up 80% or more of the plan proceeds. Talk to your attorney as to what taxes will be due on the retirement plan proceeds and what you can do now to minimize the tax bite.

HINT: You might want to increase your withdrawals from your retirement fund even though the withdrawals would be subject to income tax. You could use that money to establish a special trust to own life insurance on you. Then, the life insurance proceeds could go to your children without being subject to death tax. You would be converting a heavily taxed asset into one that is free of death tax.

How much will there be left for the kids after taxes?

QUESTION: My husband and I are leaving all of our assets directly to each other. When we're both gone, our children will inherit what's left. We are worth $1,200,000 together ($600,000 each). Is there an easy way to calculate how much will be left for our children after death taxes are paid?

There's an easy way to calculate how much *federal* death tax will be paid by the surviving spouse's estate. Take a look at the chart on page 203. The tax on $1,200,000 is $235,000.

You could make this tax go down to zero on the $1,200,000 in assets if you changed your plan to include a "death tax saving trust" (sometimes called a "B trust," "Credit Shelter trust" or "Exemption trust") at the time the first of you passed away. Then you could probably save $235,000 in federal death tax at the surviving spouse's death.

The reason your current plan would be so heavily taxed is that you are only taking advantage of the surviving spouse's $600,000 exemption from death tax. That's what happens when one spouse leaves everything outright to the surviving spouse. There's only one exemption available, the surviving spouse's, to shield the assets from federal death tax.

If the surviving spouse is worth $1,200,000 and can only shield $600,000 from death tax with one exemption, then the remaining $600,000 will be taxed.

There is a way to use both of your $600,000 exemptions and shield up to $1,200,000 from death tax. Instead of leaving everything outright to the surviving spouse, the first spouse to die could set up a death tax saving trust in a will or trust. The surviving spouse could benefit from this kind of trust and, in some cases, be the trustee (manager) of the trust. Your attorney can tell you how this type of trust works.

HINT: In addition, if needed, the surviving spouse could make lifetime gifts to reduce the death tax bite on the survivor's estate.

To really calculate how much will be left, your attorney also has to tell you how other taxes such as excise taxes, the generation-skipping tax and income tax will impact your estates. Finally, you need to know what the fees of the attorney and your executor or trustee will be on each of your deaths.

Each year you should review your asset and liability situation with your attorney to see the impact of the tax laws on your estates. You should also contact your attorney before making purchases or sales of major assets so that everything is structured correctly from the start.

By anticipating what the cash needs will be at your death, you can help plan for the best ways to meet those needs.

Ways to increase the amount that will be left for the kids after taxes

QUESTION: Are there ways to decrease the death tax bite besides using the $600,000 exemption?

Yes. There are several ways to reduce death taxes. Besides lifetime gifts, one way is to shift an "opportunity" (e.g., an investment) to your children well in advance of your death where there is a good likelihood that the opportunity will grow in value. Certain family partnership arrangements and/or lifetime transfers of interests in family businesses or property can also reduce the tax bite.

HINT: You should review this area very carefully with your estate planning attorney since there are special rules for family transactions. Failure to follow the required rules can result in a very upsetting death tax bill that exceeds the ability to pay. Death taxes are bad enough when you anticipate them. When they come out of left field, they can be overwhelming, especially at a time of grief and loss.

Finally, you should consider life insurance. There are ways to own life insurance so you can pass on huge amounts of life insurance to your children without any death tax due on the proceeds.

How much should we leave for the kids?

QUESTION: How can we calculate how much our children will need after we're gone?

Step 1 is to take a look at what you have and what you owe. Be realistic in adding up your assets and subtracting your liabilities. Savings accounts, life insurance, retirement plans and stocks can provide ready cash for your estate. For other assets such as real estate (that your children won't be living in), estimate what your assets would sell for after you're gone.

As for your liabilities, when are they due? Are there regular mortgage payments on your house or investment property that are spread out evenly over 15 years or is there a balloon (i.e., large) payment that's due next year?

Step 2 is to subtract the expected death tax, income tax, attorney's fees and executor's (or trustee's) fees that will be due.

Step 3 is to look at your children's circumstances. How much you want to have on hand for small children can be a very different story as compared to grown children who are doing okay financially on their own (a rarity these days, to be sure). Also, you may have one or more young or adult children who have special disabilities that require additional

123

resources.

What standard of living do you want your children to have? Do you want them to be able to attend private school as a youngster as well as a private college as an adult? What about money for their graduate studies, too?

Where will your young children be living if you're not around? Will the people you're naming as their guardian need to add on to their house to have your children live there, too? Are you able to provide the funding for that?

Step 4 is to take all of the information from the first three steps and work backwards to come up with the "right" amount to leave for your children.

Begin by estimating the future income from your assets. Since we don't know what the future holds in the economy, you'll probably want to experiment with different rates of return. You should pick three different rates, one high, one low and one in the middle.

Next, you should estimate how much each of your children will need per year (such as $10,000 for one child and $15,000 for another child) and build in an inflation factor on these expenses, too.

Once you calculate the expected income and expenses over the years, you'll be able to see how long your money will last. Will your money be gone before all of your children are age 21? Age 18? Age 12?

The last question is whether you want some money left over to give to your children after they attain a magic age (for example, age 21).

Use these four steps and make any necessary adjustments to calculate the sum of money you'll need to have on hand to provide for your children.

HINT: Do you need more life insurance? Life insurance may be the only way to leave enough to provide for your children's needs, especially if they're young children.

You should remember that some of the insurance proceeds may go to the IRS instead of to your children, depending upon the size of your estates and the way you own life insurance. Talk to your attorney about the ways life insurance may pass to your kids free of federal death tax.

Building flexibility into your estate plan

QUESTION: How important is it to build flexibility into our estate plan?

It may be very important, depending upon individual circumstances.

We all know that circumstances change over time. If a will or trust is drafted too rigidly, those changes may result in a distortion of the intended result.

For example, let's say that a will was signed in the late 1940s providing a $250 per month benefit to the couple's only child. This was a sizable sum at that time. Once the surviving parent died and the years went by, the daughter became disabled and unable to supplement the $250 per month benefit. The trust might have hundreds of thousands of dollars that could (and should) benefit the only child. A court might be able to rewrite the will so that the child could benefit in a way to reflect the cost of living in the 1990s.

This same scenario could take place today if you provided a child with a fixed amount such as $20,000 per year. A better way would be for the will to either have a fixed dollar amount change over time as the cost of living changed and/or give your representative (i.e., the trustee) the ability to pay out more to the child if it made sense for the child's support, health, maintenance and education.

On the other hand, you might want to limit a beneficiary's share. Let's say you wanted to leave $25,000 to your brother but everything else to the kids once your spouse and you are gone.

Do you really mean $25,000 or $25,000 if it doesn't exceed 10% of your assets? You might want to condition dollar bequests with a limitation that they do not exceed a certain portion of your estate. Otherwise, that "small" beneficiary may end up with the lion's share of your assets.

Let's look at another example. If you had two small children, you might want to divide up all of your assets equally between the children when you're both gone. That way each child could benefit from his or her share.

However, what if one child required an operation or special therapy that would cost more than the child's one-half share? If you were alive, you would pay for the operation or therapy and not worry that the other child would be inheriting less. To carry out that thinking you could have one big pot (commonly called a "family pot trust") for both children and allow them to benefit unequally from the trust until the trust is divided when, say, the youngest child attains age 21 or 25. That way your representative, your trustee, could have flexibility to look at situations as they arise and you wouldn't have to use a crystal ball to predict what might occur in the future.

Let's take another example. You might have two children, one who is wealthy today and one who is not. You might say, "I'll just leave everything to the one child who needs it." What happens if the wealthy child goes bankrupt because the housing market or the stock market falls apart? Would it have been better to set aside a certain amount that could go to either child as determined by the trustee? These rainy day trusts can be very important. You cannot depend on one child helping out the other one.

Let's look at those same two children again. You might still want to divide up your estate equally between the children with the idea that your wealthy child will give his share to his children (your grandchildren). You might want to build into your plan a *non-taxable* way for your child to voluntarily push (the technical tax word for this is "disclaim") those assets to his children.

In some cases, too much flexibility in your will or trust isn't a good idea. Let's say you die first and give your surviving spouse a limited ability to reallocate your assets among your bloodline. If your spouse has a minor spat with a child, it's possible that the child will get nothing from you or your spouse since the child could be excluded entirely. Instead, you might have minimum guaranteed amounts going to each child and give an independent person (or trust company) the ability to increase those minimums.

HINT: Don't box your estate plan into a corner that does not allow it to breathe. Your plan should have a way to meet most of the unexpected needs of your children as well as their anticipated needs.

Survival periods and saving death taxes

QUESTION: When my husband or I die, we want the other one to inherit everything. We each have $400,000 in assets making the total together around $800,000. We realize that this could cause extra death tax since the surviving spouse would be worth $800,000, which is more than the $600,000 federal death tax exemption. Knowing this, we still don't want to pay to have a will or trust prepared that might exempt up to $1,200,000 in federal death tax. Is there any inexpensive way we could each still have our $600,000 exemptions in case we died together or pretty close in time?

Probably. You might want your attorney to add a survival period to your wills or trust of say 60 days. That way, if you died within 60 days of each other, neither of you would have lived long enough to inherit from the other one. Then, each of your estates would equal $400,000 and be within the $600,000 exemption. So, if the value of your estates stayed the same, your children would not have to pay any federal death tax.

However, if one of you outlived the other one for at least 61 days and then died, then the surviving spouse's estate would be $800,000 and subject to death tax.

HINT: Have your attorney coordinate a survival period for life insurance and other benefits, too.

These same kinds of death tax issues could apply in your children's estates, too, where they inherit or benefit from you. Then, too, there's also the issue of controlling who ultimately inherits your assets.

For example, let's say you named your two children as equal beneficiaries on your life insurance policies if they outlive both of you. What if one of your children is in a car accident with you and outlives you for just a short period of time such as 10 days?

The life insurance proceeds would probably be paid one half to your living child and the other half to the estate of your deceased child. Now, the share of the child who died could have to go through a probate of the child's estate. That could mean attorney's fees, delays and a loss of control as to who would inherit from your child.

Your attitude might be, when I'm gone, who cares? However, you may feel differently if a child survives you for only a short period of time and leaves the inheritance from you to non-relatives rather than to your bloodline.

How to avoid a forced sale of assets to pay death taxes

QUESTION: My wife and I have our family business, our house, some savings accounts and a little bit in retirement plans. We know that there will be death tax due when we are both gone and there won't be enough cash on hand to pay the death tax due. We don't want our two kids to have to borrow against any of our assets to pay the death tax. Is there any way they can pay the tax and still avoid a forced sale of the business or the house?

Probably. You should consider having a life insurance policy that pays off at the time you are both gone. It's cheaper to pay for a policy that requires two deaths (your wife's and yours) rather than one. This kind of insurance policy is called a "second-to-die" policy.

Note, however, if your wife or you own or control the policy, the proceeds will be added to your taxable estate and increase the federal death tax even more. Keep in mind that if your estates will already be subject to federal death tax, then whatever is added to your estates will be taxed at a *minimum* rate of 37%.

So, you need to find a way to have the insurance proceeds available to *loan* to your estates to pay the death tax without having these insurance proceeds taxed as part of your estates. You have two possibilities to explore with your attorney. First, you should ask about the desirability of your children owning the policy. Second, you may want your attorney to prepare a special kind of trust known as a "life insurance trust" to own the policy.

HINT: If your children are young, then a life insurance trust may be the only way to go. Also, if your children are not too responsible financially, it may not be a good idea for them to own the policy and receive the proceeds directly. These are some of the factors you need to discuss with your attorney to come up with the right solution for you.

Another avenue to explore is whether your estates would qualify for the special, low-interest payment plan of federal death tax where your estate includes a closely held (family) business. There are certain requirements to be met to qualify for this special payment program.

Finally, have you given sufficient thought as to what will happen to the business when one of you or both of you are gone? Will one or both of your children want to run the business? Will they be able to do so? Do they know your main suppliers, customers and competition? If they needed or wanted to sell the business, would they know how to proceed? You might want to have a written set of instructions together with a video or audio tape explaining the most important aspects of the business. Your guided tour of the business could be viewed after you're gone so that your children would know how to maximize the benefit of your estate. As with anything related to your estate plan, make sure you keep things up to date and that your attorney is aware, in advance, of the steps you plan to take.

Lifetime gifts may increase income tax

QUESTION: I'm an 80 year old widow. I have one child whom I love dearly. Since I fell ill a few years ago, I've been living with him and his wife who treat me like a queen. I am thinking of giving my son all of my stocks right now. That's all I have in the way of assets. When my husband died many years ago, he left me very little. I had to go back to work. I saved my money and bought these stocks from my earnings. Although I paid $100,000 for the stocks, they are worth $400,000 now. Will a gift now save taxes?

Probably not. A gift now will probably increase federal taxes. The tax increase would be an increase in *income* tax, not an increase in death tax or gift tax.

Since your net worth is below $600,000, you could give your son the stocks now and pay *no* federal gift tax. If, instead, your son inherited the stocks from you, he could receive stocks worth up to $600,000 with *no* federal death tax. Thus, with regard to gift or death tax, it doesn't make any federal tax difference whether your son gets the stocks during your lifetime or after you're gone.

The big tax difference is in federal income tax. To understand this difference, you need to understand the concept of "income tax basis."

An income tax basis is the starting point for calculating gain or loss. Generally, it's what you paid for an asset.

First, let's take a look at how income tax basis works while you're alive. Since you paid $100,000 for the stocks, that's your income tax basis. If you sold the stocks now for $400,000, you would have made a profit or gain. Your gain would be $300,000. The way you calculate your gain is to determine the difference between what you'd receive ($400,000) less what you paid (which is your income tax basis or $100,000 in this case). Then, you'd pay income tax on the difference ($300,000 in this case) at your income tax rate.

Next, let's take a look at what happens when you make a gift during your lifetime. In general, the person receiving the gift (your son in this case) steps into your shoes as far as the income tax basis. So, if your income tax basis were $100,000, then his basis would be the same. If your son sold the stocks for $400,000, then he would have a $300,000 gain, too. This would be true whether he sold the stocks for $400,000 during your lifetime or after you're gone.

Finally, let's take a look at how the tax rules are different when, with certain exceptions, someone inherits from you instead of receiving the asset from you while you are alive.

The person inheriting (your son) gets a *new* federal income tax basis equal to what the stocks were worth when you passed away. This rule applies to most assets but not to IRAs or most retirement plans.

The new income tax basis upon a death can make a big difference for your son's income tax. If the stocks were worth $400,000 at the time of your death and your son inherited them, he could sell them for $400,000 and pay *no* federal income tax. Why? Because *when one inherits after someone else dies, the one who inherits get a new federal tax income basis. That income tax basis is equal to what the asset was worth when the person giving the inheritance died.*

HINT: Talk to your attorney before making any gifts. See if the proposed gift will save taxes or cost taxes. Before making any gifts, your attorneys needs to discuss with you the implications for federal and state income tax, federal and state gift tax, federal death tax, state inheritance tax and state and local property tax.

You should also ask about whether a probate will be required if you do not make a lifetime gift.

Finally, you should ask how a transfer of assets during your lifetime might make sense to protect the assets against future medical bills.

Community property

QUESTION: My husband and I own certain assets as community property and other assets as joint tenancy. Our wills either leave everything to each other or we have a trust for the surviving spouse. I can't remember. Anyway, should we care whether our assets are held as community property or in joint tenancy?

Yes. How you hold title could affect four main things: 1) federal death tax, 2) who will ultimately inherit your assets, 3) whether a probate is required and 4) the amount of federal income tax.

As you read on, keep in mind that only certain states in the U.S. allow community property as a way of owning assets and only a husband and wife can own assets as community property.

Federal death tax on the first death

In general, for federal death tax purposes, it does not matter at the *first death* whether spouses hold title as community property or as joint tenancy if the surviving spouse is to inherit everything under a will.

When a husband or wife dies, one-half of community property assets are included in the taxable estate of the spouse who died. The same is generally true for assets held in joint tenancy. For example, if a husband and wife own $400,000 in assets together as community property *or* in joint tenancy, then the taxable estate of the first spouse to pass away will be $200,000.

Federal death tax on the surviving spouse's death

When spouses hold assets in joint tenancy and one spouse dies, the surviving spouse ends up owning 100 percent of the assets. That can mean that the survivor's estate may be pushed over the $600,000 federal death tax exemption. If the survivor's estate exceeds the exemption, there will be less for the children since more death tax will be due at the survivor's death.

Assets held with a spouse in joint tenancy automatically go to the surviving spouse upon a death. Assets held with a spouse as community property, however, do *not* automatically go to the surviving spouse upon a death though it may turn out that way. With community property, you look to the will or trust of the spouse who died to see who gets the one-half interest of the deceased spouse. The other half still belongs to the surviving spouse of course.

Just as with joint tenancy, if the will of the first to die leaves community property assets directly to the surviving spouse, then the surviving spouse will end up owning all of the assets. This, of course, will increase the chances that death tax will be due.

If, instead, a death tax saving trust has been made part of a will or trust, then joint tenancy and community property *can* produce different death tax results upon the surviving spouse's death.

If a death tax saving trust has been established, joint tenancy can cause more death tax to be paid on the *surviving spouse's* death than if their assets had been held as community property. The reason for this is that for a death tax saving trust to work, there needs to be assets in the trust. Otherwise, the trust that was set up to save death tax has nothing in it. The emptiness of the trust eliminates the benefit of the tax planning of the trust. Joint tenancy assets automatically go directly to the surviving spouse and not to the death tax saving trust. This results in the surviving spouse's estate being larger and more likely to be taxed.

With community property, one half of the community property on the first death can automatically go to a death tax saving trust set up under a will or trust rather than directly to a surviving spouse. Thus, there are assets in the death tax saving trust which reduces the size of the surviving spouse's estate. In a properly written death tax saving trust, the assets in that trust are not counted in the survivor's taxable estate for federal death tax purposes. With a death tax saving trust that contains assets of the first to die, the children save death tax upon the surviving spouse's death.

Who will ultimately inherit your assets?

Since joint tenancy assets go directly to the surviving spouse and do not pass under a will or trust, the first spouse to die has lost control as to who will ultimately inherit those assets from the surviving spouse. The surviving spouse can leave the assets to anyone, including a new spouse.

However, with the first to die's share of *community property assets* left to a trust, the first to die can name who will ultimately inherit his or her share of the remaining assets.

Will there be a probate on the first death?

Barring a simultaneous death of both spouses, joint tenancy assets pass automatically to the surviving joint tenant (in this case the surviving spouse) without having to go through a court probate. Community property assets, however, *may* have to go through a probate or a less involved court proceeding when the first spouse dies. This can increase the costs and attorney's fees after a death as compared to joint tenancy.

Will there be a probate on the second death?

Without advance planning to avoid probate, there may be a probate on the survivor's death whether the assets are held in joint tenancy or community property.

Will federal income tax be the same for the surviving spouse with joint tenancy as compared to community property?

Probably not. The difference, in general, is apparent when the surviving spouse sells assets that had previously been owned together.

In some cases, joint tenancy will save federal income tax and in other cases community property will save federal income tax.

Federal income tax may be higher or lower depending on a) which way spouses hold title to a particular asset, b) the purchase price of the asset, c) what the asset will be worth at the time the first spouse passes away and d) what the asset will be sold for (if it's sold) by the surviving spouse.

The general rule of thumb is that 1) if an asset has gone up or will probably go up in value after the date of purchase, hold it as community property (if it's possible in the state where the property is located), and 2) if an asset has gone down or will probably go down in value after the date of purchase, do *not* hold it as community property.

The reasoning behind the general rule of thumb is that the *survivor's one-half interest* in assets is treated differently under the federal income tax rules after one spouse dies, depending upon whether an asset was held in joint tenancy or as community property.

With community property, the federal income tax basis of the survivor's half interest is revised to whatever the fair market value is when the first spouse dies. With joint tenancy, nothing changes as to the federal income tax basis of the survivor's half.

With either joint tenancy or community property, the *one-half interest of the spouse who dies first* is treated the same for income tax purposes. The federal income tax basis of that one-half interest is revised to whatever the fair market value is when the first spouse dies.

Let's look at how the general rule would apply for an asset

141

that had gone up in value between the date of purchase and the date of the first spouse's death.

For example, assume John Dough and Jane Dough, a married couple, bought a house for $100,000 and it's worth $400,000 at the time the first spouse (John) passes away. If Jane as the surviving spouse later sells the house for $400,000, the income tax effect is far different depending upon whether John and Jane held title as community property or as joint tenants while they were both alive.

If the house were worth $400,000 at the time of John's death and the property were held as *community property*, then the starting point for Jane to have any federal income tax gain on a sale of the house would be $400,000. In other words, under community property, Jane could pocket the first $400,000 in sale proceeds free of any federal income tax. There would be no capital gain on the sale.

With community property, 100 percent of an asset gets a new starting point (a new "federal income tax basis") equal to what the asset was worth when John died ($400,000).

With joint tenancy, only the half interest owned by John gets a new starting point for federal income tax purposes. That new starting point would be one-half of $400,000 which equals $200,000. Jane's one-half interest remains at what she paid for the asset (one-half of $100,000 which equals $50,000).

With joint tenancy in this example, Jane would have a gain on a sale of the house above $250,000 ($200,000 for the half owned by John plus $50,000 for Jane's half). In other words, with joint tenancy Jane could pocket only the first $250,000 in sale proceeds free of any federal income tax.

So, the income tax basis for 100 percent of the house after John's death is $400,000 with community property and $250,000 ($200,000 plus $50,000) with joint tenancy.

Note, however, that this is not a one-way street. Community property can have its income tax downside, too. If an asset goes down in value, then community property could end up costing the surviving spouse additional income tax on a sale.

With either joint tenancy or community property, the surviving spouse may also be able to exclude gain through the once-in-a-lifetime exclusion of $125,000 of gain which is available to some taxpayers.

HINT: Even if you live in a "community property state," your assets may not be community property. You may need to sign a written agreement or other document to have title to the assets be considered as community property.

Also, as everyone becomes more mobile and moves around the country, it's possible that you'll be taking community property assets such as pensions and retirement plans from one state into a non-community property state. Those assets may remain community property which may affect who ultimately receives them. Ask your attorney if community property issues will impact your estate.

Naming charities in wills and trusts to reduce death tax

QUESTION: My wife and I have done well financially. We have more than enough to help out our kids. If we leave some of our estate to charities, will that reduce death taxes?

In general, yes. Amounts you leave to charities approved by the IRS are deductible by your estate. You can reduce the death tax bite and benefit charities at the same time.

There are also ways to benefit your spouse and/or children first and then have the balance go to charity after they're all gone.

HINT: Ask your attorney if any death tax will be paid out of the charity's share. Sometimes extra (and unnecessary) death tax is paid which reduces the amount going to charity.

If you are concerned about too much of your estate going to charity and not enough to your children, you might obtain a new life insurance policy owned by your children or by an "irrevocable trust" (a trust you cannot change after it's created). Done correctly, the proceeds from this life insurance policy would escape death tax and increase the amount going to your children.

Depending upon the amount of life insurance, you might want to insure with more than one insurance company just in case a life insurance company has a financial problem that's not covered by a state insurance fund. Ask your insurance agent how the independent rating companies view the financial health of the insurance companies you're considering.

Lifetime gifts to charities

QUESTION: My husband and I want to sell an investment property and give the proceeds to a certain charity. The problem is that the amount we actually give to the charity will be reduced by the income tax on the sale of the property. And, we'd really like to keep some of the income from the sale of the property. Any ideas?

Yes. You should talk to your attorney about giving the property to the charity and letting the charity sell the property. The charity won't pay income tax on the sale since it's a tax-exempt entity. You could receive a current income tax deduction for your gift to the charity.

Also, instead of just giving the property away completely, you could get arrange with the charity to establish an annuity so you could get monthly income from the sales proceeds. The charity would receive the full benefit of your gift after you're gone.

There are many rules in this area and it is very complicated, especially if there is any debt on the property.

HINT: If you want to replenish your estate to replace the asset you've given away to charity, life insurance may be the answer. It's possible for life insurance proceeds to escape federal death tax.

Making bigger lifetime gifts exempt from taxes

QUESTION: I am divorced. I have two children in college. I want to give each of them more than $10,000 per calendar year without using up any part of my $600,000 exemption from death tax. Do you have a magic solution for me?

It's not magic but talk to your attorney about how, in addition to your annual $10,000 checks to them, you might write checks directly to the college to pay for your children's tuition and directly to your children's doctors for medical expenses. This may be a way to increase your gifts without using up any portion of your $600,000 federal exemption.

HINT: Ask your attorney whether there might be any *state* gift tax due as a result of these gifts.

Less tax may be paid on lifetime gifts as compared to inheritances

QUESTION: I recently sold most of my real estate. Even after income tax, I have plenty of cash. I want to make large cash gifts to my kids now so they can enjoy the gifts. My estate is large enough that there will be federal death tax when I pass away. Will there be any savings in death or gift tax if I make gifts now as compared to giving it to my kids under my will?

Probably yes. The answer might be different for smaller estates. Although federal gift tax and federal death tax share the same $600,000 exemption, the way the taxes are calculated is different. The bottom line is that if your assets exceed the $600,000 exemption, you can give away more through lifetime gifts and pay less tax than through inheritances at death. Of course, it is not always wise to make lifetime gifts. Before you do so, just be sure that at some later date you won't need the assets you've given away.

HINT: You need to discuss your entire situation with your attorney to see what size lifetime gifts make sense for your overall estate plan. You also need to have your attorney discuss with you the state tax rules, too.

Can moving to another state affect taxes?

QUESTION: I'm thinking of moving to another state to retire. I already signed a will a few years ago. Is there anything I should be thinking about in connection with this possible move?

You should be advised as to the death tax, income tax and property tax laws in the new state *before* you move.

HINT: Don't assume that all of the laws and taxes in each state are the same. If you do move, you should also have an attorney in the new home state take a look at your will and trust to see if anything needs to be changed.

Can your burial site affect taxes?

QUESTION: I have residences in two states. One of the states has a very high inheritance tax rate and the other one does not (where I live most of the time). I want to be buried in the family plot which is in the state with higher death taxes. Could this lead to the higher taxing state or both states trying to tax my estate?

Maybe. You can't even rest in peace.

You can have more than one residence but you can only have one "domicile." In general, your domicile is the state where you have your permanent home to which you always intend to return (during your lifetime).

Your selection of a burial site may influence the determination of your domicile. You should talk to your attorney about how to establish a domicile for tax purposes and how the inheritance laws work in the various states with which you have a connection. Otherwise, more than one state may try to tax your estate, especially if it's a large estate.

HINT: Don't assume that all of the laws and taxes in each state are the same. Whenever you have assets or connections in more than one state, you need to alert your attorney to the situation.

Are joint wills between husband and wife a good idea?

QUESTION: My wife and I signed a joint will, that is, we both signed the same will covering what happens when each of us dies. Is there any problem with this?

Probably. Joint wills can have some unexpected income tax effects when one of you dies. Talk to your attorney about your joint will.

HINT: The main attraction of joint wills is locking everything into place in a way that cannot be changed after one spouse dies. This can be a real disadvantage due to the lack of flexibility for the surviving spouse. Talk to your attorney about whether the surviving spouse should have some limited flexibility in case circumstances change. For example, years after the first of you passes away, it might make sense to reallocate your assets among your children due to their changed circumstances. Will your hands be tied due to a joint will? Again, talk to your attorney.

PART FIVE

SPECIAL
SITUATIONS

Divorced parents with minor children

QUESTION: My husband and I were divorced three years ago. Our sons are ages 5 and 10. I've set up trusts that take care of my children after my death. Everything is divided equally between them at the time of my death and kept in separate trusts. Until they are age 21, their support, maintenance and educational needs are to be taken care of from my assets. At age 21, they will each receive their share of the remaining assets. I have not changed title to my assets or my beneficiary designations since my divorce. Have I taken care of everything to protect my children?

Probably not. Consider the following scenario: If you pass away and one of your children passes away (as a youngster) before age 21, have you specified who inherits the assets in that child's trust? If the trust names the child's estate as the recipient, then your deceased child's closest relative, possibly your ex-spouse, could inherit as the closest relative.

You want to be sure to name a contingent beneficiary in case any child passes away before receiving his entire trust. You may want to name your other son or, possibly, any then living children of your deceased child.

Next, let's imagine that you pass away many years from now and your children are adults. If your children inherit from you and then they pass away, what will happen to the assets they inherited? If they do not leave a will or trust and do not have a spouse or child of their own, your ex-spouse might inherit in that case, too. State law may say that your child's closest relative, the child's father (your ex-spouse), will inherit all of a child's assets (including what your child inherited from you).

HINT: Instead of leaving assets outright and in the pockets of your children, you might want to put some strings on the assets such as creating trusts for them that last longer than age 21 or age 25.

Be sure to talk to your attorney about naming guardians for your minor children, too. Even if your ex-spouse is appointed as the guardian to raise the children, you may be able to name your own choice for the guardian who will be handling the *assets* you're leaving to the children.

Finally, be sure to see how you hold title to your assets and check your beneficiary designations on your life insurance, retirement plans and IRAs so that your children, not your ex-spouse, inherit the assets. In some states, your ex-spouse would automatically be removed as a possible beneficiary.

Even if your ex-spouse would always do the right thing by the kids, why take any chances? What would happen if your ex-spouse remarries, is still named as beneficiary under your life insurance and dies shortly after you? Would the new spouse of your ex-spouse be generous towards your kids in turning over the life insurance proceeds due to your ex-spouse's estate? You only get one guess on this one.

Divorced (or I think they'll be divorced) adult children

QUESTION: I think my son's marriage will end up in a divorce in the next few years. He and his wife have two children. My health isn't too good. My will leaves everything to my son. Could my daughter-in-law ever end up with my assets?

Yes, it's possible unless you make some changes to your will. You should talk to your attorney about how a trust for your son could be designed to protect the assets and keep them within your bloodline, whether there's a divorce or not.

HINT: If you leave assets outright to your children with no strings attached, you lose control over what will eventually happen to those assets. The way to put conditions, or strings, on assets is to have them in a trust. Talk to your attorney as to whether a trust for your offspring makes sense in your case.

Second marriages and protecting the children of first marriages

QUESTION: I am a widower who was blessed to find some-one I'm about to marry. We each have our own assets that we want to go to our own kids from our prior marriages. We do not want any of our assets to go to each other. Do we need to do anything legal to make this happen?

Yes. You should each talk to your own separate attorneys about a premarital agreement as well as wills or trusts needed to carry out your wishes.

HINT: Before you decide to give the other spouse nothing, think about a couple of things.

Maybe you *do* want to make some provision for your surviving spouse. Let's say you were both living in a condo owned by you. Would you want your spouse to have to move out right after your death or would you want her to have some time to live there and plan her next move? Would she be paying rent or taking care of expenses on the condo during that time period? What about the furniture and furnishings in the condo? If they had belonged to you, would you want your wife left without a stick of furniture?

To ensure that you come up with the right plan, think about the logistics after a death and the financial reality of your individual situation.

Over time, you may decide to be more generous to each other in your will or trust. Rather than leaving assets outright to the surviving spouse, you may want to have a death tax saving trust (see page 121) and/or a QTIP trust (see pages 106 and 161) for the assets benefitting the surviving spouse. Then, while your surviving spouse will benefit from your assets, what's left over of your assets will ultimately go to your children.

Otherwise, if everything goes outright to your spouse (such as by holding title to assets in joint tenancy with your spouse), your children from a prior marriage may end up with nothing and *your spouse's children* may get *your assets* as well as your spouse's.

Second marriages and benefitting the second spouse

QUESTION: I married my second wife ten years ago. I have three wonderful children from my first marriage. I have a problem. If something happened to me, my wife would have nothing to live on. Is there any way I can provide for my wife and still name my children as the beneficiaries after she's gone?

Yes. There is a type of trust called a "QTIP trust" (see page 106) that allows a surviving spouse to benefit and helps protect the ultimate inheritance for your children. One way it helps protect your children is that whatever is left over after your spouse is gone goes to the beneficiaries you've named, not the beneficiaries of your spouse.

HINT: In your will or trust, you'll spell out exactly how generous this trust will be to your spouse. A QTIP trust gives your spouse at least all of the income of the trust.

If you want to be more generous, the trust can also say it's okay for trust assets to pay for your spouse's health, support and maintenance. This approach, of course, could result in nothing being left for your children. You need to balance your generosity to your spouse with your desire to leave an inheritance to your children.

Protecting governmental aid for special beneficiaries

QUESTION: We have two children. Both of them are adults. Our daughter is permanently disabled and she needs the governmental assistance she's currently receiving to live on. However, she is not able to manage her money. Our son is doing okay. Right now, our will leaves all of our assets fifty-fifty outright to our two children when we're both gone. When we're both gone, will our daughter lose her governmental aid?

It depends upon the type of governmental assistance program helping your daughter. With some programs, your daughter's benefits are unaffected. With other programs, an inheritance from you could cause her to lose her benefits.

If your daughter's governmental assistance would be lost by her inheriting from you, you have three main alternatives to consider: 1) disinheriting your daughter, 2) setting up a "special needs trust" or 3) setting up a discretionary trust.

The correct alternative depends upon a number of factors including the laws in your state and your daughter's state, the level of your wealth, the dependability of close relatives and friends and the personal circumstances of your child, the "special beneficiary."

Disinheritance

First, and most drastic, you could disinherit your daughter

and leave everything to your son with the hope that he would do the right thing for your daughter.

There are several risks with this approach. Even if your son would do the right thing, what happens to your money when your son passes away or if he becomes disabled while your daughter is still alive? How will your daughter be taken care of?

With a disinheritance, you have literally passed the buck to the recipient (for example, your son) to set up the appropriate plan to take care of your daughter.

Special needs trust

Second, you could keep the share for your daughter in a trust known as a "special needs trust." Some states allow you to set up a special needs trust to benefit your child without losing certain types of governmental aid.

With a special needs trust, a formula is used to spell out what's permitted to be spent for your child. Such trusts often say that benefits may only be paid to or for your child as a supplement to governmental aid to the extent the benefits from the trust do not disqualify your child from any aid program.

The reason a formula is used rather than dollar amounts is that the permitted benefits allowed by the government will change over time. If you put dollar amounts in the trust document, the safe dollar amount today may be a forbidden, excessive amount in the future.

With a special needs trust, your child has no *right* to any income from the trust or to its principal. Instead, the purposes for which money may be spent for your child are very limited. It is the lack of rights for your child that protects the trust. The reason for this is that if the government attacks the trust, it gets to step into the shoes of your child. Whatever your child is entitled to, the government is entitled to since it is supporting your child. The more remote your child's interest is in the trust, the less of a chance the government will claim any interest on the child's behalf.

You might decide to divide up your estate unevenly between your children if you're using a special needs trust since the permitted benefits are relatively small.

Remember that this technique is not 100 percent guaranteed anywhere since laws can change over time. This could be a problem because you are setting up a plan for your daughter that will last as long as she is alive.

You may also have a problem morally using such a trust to keep assets away from the government. Should your estate pay the government back for the aid provided to your adult child? That's your decision. Is this any different than utilizing a tax benefit that's available to you?

Discretionary trust

The third main alternative is to use a "discretionary trust." This type of trust is used more often when your estate is larger. It's a pay-for-yourself approach as compared to the governmental aid approach of the special needs trust.

With a discretionary trust, the trustee has total discretion to spend or not spend money of the trust for your child. The purposes for which money can be spent are not as restrictive as with a special needs trust. Very often you'll allow the trustee to pay for any of your child's needs for health, maintenance, support and education (and sometimes other language is added such as "for care and comfort").

HINT: You should talk to your attorney about the wisdom of establishing a special needs trust for your child. Your decision will depend upon the level of your wealth, the financial circumstances of each of your children, the relationship between your children and the desirability of keeping governmental aid.

With a special needs trust, there are other steps to consider to help protect the trust against a governmental attack. If you have another current beneficiary of the trust whose rights are not so restricted (for example, a sibling to the special beneficiary), it would be harder for the government to attack the trust. The reason for this is that it would be more difficult for the government to claim that all or maybe even most of the trust assets would or should ever go to the special beneficiary.

With any kind of trust for your children, think about naming an advocate for each of your children, sort of a guardian angel, who could make sure the trustee is treating your children properly.

Your trust document might also state that your assets would pay for the legal expenses incurred by the advocate if the advocate felt a court action had to be brought to protect your children (whether the advocate won or lost).

When you pick an advocate (or for that matter, any representative of your estate or trust), consider whether there could be any conflict of interest. Does your will or trust say that the unspent assets in your child's trust go to the advocate or trustee when your child dies? If that's the case, perhaps the trustee will be more stingy with expenses for your child.

You may need more than a trustee to manage your assets for your child who's a special beneficiary. You may also need someone to act as a substitute or proxy parent.

In California, a new program to explore is the Proxy Parent Services Foundation (1336 Wilshire Blvd., 2nd floor, Los Angeles, CA 90017-1705, 213/413-1130). Proxy Parent is 1) building a network of service professionals who can act in your place to provide personal care for your children and 2) acting as a liaison with a professional trust company that serves as the trustee to manage assets. Another good source of information is the National Alliance for the Mentally Ill (2101 Wilson Blvd., Suite 302, Arlington, VA 22201, 703/524-7600).

In the case of a special needs trust, whomever you name as the ultimate beneficiary may help protect the trust.

If a charity is the ultimate beneficiary of the special needs trust, then an attack by the government on the trust could result in taking money away from a charity. That would not be a very popular action to take.

Are the rights of creditors affected by how I hold title?

QUESTION: I'm doing okay financially at this time. However, in this economy I'm worried about a financial reversal. Do creditors have stronger or weaker claims to my assets if I hold title to my assets in joint tenancy or a living trust?

In general, setting up a living trust provides no protection against creditors. Since you can revoke the trust and maintain total control over your assets, you are considered to still own the assets while you are alive. At your death, the assets in the trust are usually subject to claims by your creditors.

It may be, however, that holding title as a joint tenant gives more creditor protection to your surviving joint tenant after you're gone. State law will determine if that's the case.

There are types of *irrevocable trusts*, however, that may provide better protection against creditors.

Having said all of this, of course, I'm sure you would want all of your obligations paid. Talk to your attorney about how creditors would get paid after you're gone.

HINT: The rights of creditors after you're gone are affected by what you do during your lifetime. To maximize protection against creditors, you should find out the best way to hold title to

your assets and whom to name as the beneficiary on your life insurance, retirement plans
and IRAs. For example, you might inadvert-
ently give creditors rights to otherwise exempt
assets if your beneficiary designations were to
be completed one way as compared to another. Talk to your attorney about this issue.

Surviving spouses who are not U.S. citizens

QUESTION: My husband and I did our wills and living trust in 1987. We are each worth over $600,000 so we made sure our wills contained trusts to produce no death tax when one of us dies. By the way, we are permanent residents, not U.S. citizens. Since nothing much has changed with us since our wills were prepared, is there any point to seeing an attorney to review our wills?

Yes. The federal tax rules have changed for any surviving spouse who is not a U.S. citizen.

Under these new rules, there will be a death tax imposed when one of you dies unless you amend your plan to meet the new requirements. The trusts that comply with the new rules are called QDOTs (qualified domestic trusts).

HINT: When you talk to your attorney about updating your estate plan, make sure that your beneficiary designations on life insurance, retirement plans and IRAs are reviewed, too. Also, explore establishing a life insurance trust (see pages 24, 122 and 131-133) for death tax reasons.

Co-ownership of assets with friends and acquaintances

QUESTION: I own three houses with my best friend, Joe. We own the houses fifty-fifty. Joe has two grown children and I have three small ones. Joe is married and I'm divorced. If something happened to Joe or me, the survivor wouldn't want to co-own the houses with each other's children. Joe and I trust each other's judgment and integrity completely. Besides working out what we should do and sealing it with a handshake, what else can we do?

It sounds like you'll want to talk to your attorney about having a written agreement. The exact type of agreement may be one of many alternatives, depending upon all of your goals and the relative cost of putting those goals in writing. You're probably looking at having a buy/sell agreement that spells out what happens when one or both of you dies. Instead, you might have a "partnership agreement" or perhaps a "right of first refusal agreement" wherein the survivor is given the option, or first right, to buy the half interest owned by the deceased partner.

HINT: The issues you are raising are not limited to death situations. Be thinking about provisions dealing with disability, too. Make sure any provision where one of you can buy out the other is realistic in its purchase price and payment terms and that it remains realistic over time.

171

Depending upon how you hold title with friends, the friends, and not your loved ones, may inherit those assets. That's because you may hold title in a way that overrides your will or trust so that your share automatically passes to the other person on title. You should have your attorney check how you hold title to your assets with friends.

To add insult to injury, it's possible that your loved ones would have to pay the death tax on the assets going to your friend.

Finally, make sure your attorney takes into account the death tax issues in the agreement. Depending upon how the agreement reads, the actual "buy-out proceeds" your children receive may be far less than how the IRS values (and taxes) the properties.

Co-ownership of assets with family members

QUESTION: To reduce death taxes, I want to shift some of my assets to my three children now. Even though only one of my children works in the family business, I'm thinking of giving all of them some stock in my business. I'm also thinking of making joint investments with one of my children. Should I talk to my attorney first?

Yes. In the last few years, Congress has passed laws that set stringent guidelines and rules for gifts to and investments with children. If you do not find out in advance what the do's and dont's are, your estate will be in for a big surprise and you may end up defeating the entire purpose of your actions.

HINT: What may seem like a routine transaction or action to you can have tremendous, unforeseen tax consequences. The world is very complex these days, probably too complex. However, it's always easier to find a way around an obstacle if you're not already mired in it. Planning (particularly advance planning) is a very good idea especially when you're involving your children in the equation.

There are special tax rules for certain types of corporations known as "S Corporations." Many small corporations are S Corporations. Ask your attorney whether your corporation is or qualifies as an S Corporation. Make sure that any transfer of stock by you does not disqualify the corporation from these special tax benefits.

Consider the non-tax consequences, too. First, ask your attorney what rights your children will have in "your" corporation once they become stockholders.

Second, since you have three children and only one of them is active in the business, should they be co-owners of the business now or in the future?

Will the non-active children resent the active one receiving what they consider to be too high a salary that leaves little in the way of profit for them?

Will one or more of your children want to sell their shares to outsiders without giving the other children a chance to match any outside offer? Will you want to restrict their ability to do so with a written agreement?

Maybe you should only give stock in the business now to the one child who's active in the business and also leave the business just to that child. In that case, you'd want to leave other, compensating assets to the other children. Of course, that's not always possible. However, life insurance may be the way to equalize the inheritances.

To have a coordinated and proper plan, you'll want to discuss these items with your attorney as well as the terms of your will or trust.

Gay parents

QUESTION: I am a gay man. I have two grown children from my former marriage. I have been in a loving relationship for over ten years now. My children have a great relationship with me and my lover. My intent is to leave personal items to my lover but all of the rest of my assets to my children. Right now everything I own is held in joint tenancy with my lover. Do I need to sign a will or do anything else to put things in order?

Yes. You'll want to sign a will or trust spelling out who gets what. You'll also need to revise the ownership designation (i.e., the title) of your assets so that they are no longer held in joint tenancy. Joint tenancy usually means that the surviving joint tenant (your lover) would get assets held with him even if your will or trust reads differently. At best there would be confusion and ill feelings. At worst, your intended result will not occur, everyone will pay tremendous legal fees and everyone will probably feel hurt.

HINT: Even if you trust your lover completely, consider this scenario: There's a car accident in which you pass away first and your lover passes away the next day. So, he's the surviving joint tenant.

Who will inherit the joint assets? Unless you take the necessary preventative steps, your family may be left out entirely.

176

Gay children

QUESTION: My wife and I have three sons and four grand-children. Our two oldest children are married and our youngest child is gay and in a relationship. How can we make sure our grandchildren (and not our daughters-in-law or our son's lover) ultimately inherit our estates so everything stays in our blood-line? Is there anything special we need to do for each of our children in our wills to accomplish that result?

Actually the issue is the same for all of your children. You do not want your assets to go outside your bloodline. You only want your children, grandchildren and great-grand-children to receive your assets after you're gone.

The way to control assets after you're gone is to put strings on the assets. You put strings on assets by having a trust (under your will or trust) to hold, administer and distribute the assets during your children's lifetimes. You may be set-ting up a trust under a trust.

You'll probably want separate trusts that benefit each child and ultimately his or her then living bloodline (if any, and if there are none, then back up to your then living bloodline). You may also need to have trusts for your grandchildren to make sure the assets don't ever leave your bloodline.

HINT: If you leave assets outright to your children, you have no assurance where they will end up. You can establish trusts that benefit your children but allow you some control as to where those assets will end up. Whether your children are married, not married, gay, not gay, is irrelevant if your only concern is that children, grandchildren, great-grandchildren are to benefit.

Having such trusts for your children can also help prevent difficulties that may arise in the event of a divorce or other family break-up.

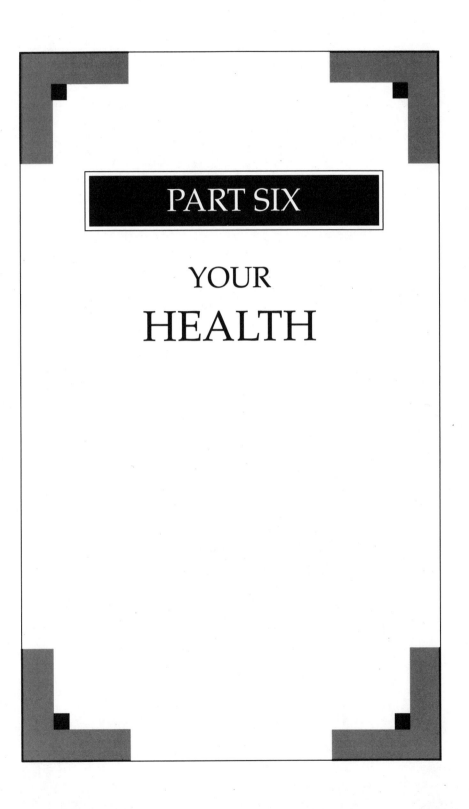

PART SIX

YOUR

HEALTH

Who will be in charge of your day-to-day living decisions if you become incapacitated?

QUESTION: I am a widow. I have two sons. I have a wonderful relationship with one of my sons, John, but things aren't going so great with my other son, Bill. If I became incapacitated, I would only want John making decisions for me, such as where I should be living. How can I make sure John will be in charge?

You'll want to sign a document spelling out who your representative will be if you should become incapacitated. You should provide for alternate choices in case the first person you have in mind can not or will not serve.

HINT: Think about whether you might want two people to make decisions jointly for you rather than relying on the judgment of just one of them.

Since a representative acting on your behalf would be entitled to a fee for the services provided to you, this kind of situation often brings relatives out of the woodwork who are not close to you.

While you are still competent, you should spell out your choices in a document (a "nomination of conservator" or "nomination of guardian" as the case may be) so a court could carry out your desires should it ever become necessary.

Who will be in charge of your money and other assets if you become incapacitated?

QUESTION: I am a widower. I have one child who's an adult. He isn't very good at handling money. If I became incapacitated, who would be in charge of my money and other assets?

That depends. You can sign documents before you become incapacitated to designate your choices. Different documents have their pluses and minuses.

You need to talk to your attorney now about how a "living trust," a "power of attorney" and a "nomination of conservator" would work if you became incapacitated.

HINT: A living trust or power of attorney usually avoids the court system altogether. The advantage is that it can be less expensive to have the representative you've named in the documents put in charge of your assets if there is no need to go through the court system. The disadvantage is that there is not a court system looking over the shoulder of the person handling your assets. This may not be a problem if you are appointing trustworthy people to handle assets for you.

Think about having two people acting together instead of one person being in charge of your money and other assets. If something happened to one of your two representatives, you might want another co-representative appointed rather than having one person act alone.

Whom you choose to manage your assets on your behalf while you are alive and incapacitated may differ from whom you want in charge after you are gone.

Pulling the plug rather than living on machines

QUESTION: My father was kept alive on machines for a long time and he was in great pain. I want to avoid that happening to me. What can I do to avoid the prolonging of life if I have a terminal illness and the pain and lack of quality outweigh the benefits?

You need to express your desires before you're unable to speak for yourself. The best way is to have a written document that spells out what you want done and what you do not want done in a terminal-illness situation.

There are two basic documents for you to explore: 1) a "health power of attorney" and 2) a "living will" (also sometimes called a "directive to physician" or "natural death declaration").

A health power of attorney appoints an agent to decide big and small health care decisions if you cannot speak for yourself. The biggest decision, of course, is whether to pull the plug (i.e., to be taken off life support machines). A lesser decision might be to choose between two possible operations where you are unconscious but not in a life-threatening situation.

You need to trust the agent you are naming completely. You should consider whether that person has any financial conflict of interest. For example, will that person inherit from you if the plug is pulled for you? Since the people you select as your agent usually inherit from you too, you should not rule out those persons just because of their status as a beneficiary. However, keep this possible conflict in mind. Also, be sure that the persons you select do not have personal or religious beliefs that will prevent them from carrying out your wishes.

The "living will" deals just with the big issue, pulling the plug. This natural death declaration is usually put into effect if you have an incurable and irreversible condition that has been diagnosed by two physicians and the condition either a) will result in your death within a relatively short time without the administration of life-sustaining treatment or b) has produced an irreversible coma or persistent vegetative state in which you are no longer able to make decisions regarding your medical treatment. Under such circumstances, a living will directs your attending physician to withhold or withdraw treatment that only prolongs an irreversible coma, a persistent vegetative state or the process of dying. Such treatment is defined as "not necessary for your comfort or to alleviate pain" and could include the use of a respirator as well as artificially administered nutrition and hydration.

HINT: You should consider having both a health power of attorney (see page 184) and a living will. If you travel a lot or have residences in more than one state, you should ask your attorney about signing forms in more than one state since states usually have their own forms.

How can I prevent the loss of my life savings if I face a long-term medical problem that exceeds my health insurance benefits?

QUESTION: We're retired. We have our house, a pension and some savings. We have one child who's an adult. Will we lose everything if one of us has a stroke or other illness that requires long-term care?

That depends. There are certain exemptions under the law and certain steps you can take if you face this situation.

Some of the steps your attorney may recommend could include a transfer of assets to your child, purchasing and/or transferring "exempt assets" under the Medicaid rules, setting up a "Medicaid trust" or petitioning a court for a higher amount of resources allowable to a spouse.

HINT: The right answer for you depends upon your exact financial and family circumstances. All of the strategies have some drawback, which may or may not be that important in your particular case.

You should find an attorney who is knowledgeable in "elder law." Before taking any recommended step, ask what the worst and most likely results would be from taking 1) the recommended action and 2) no action.

Can moving to another state affect assets if there's a long-term medical problem?

QUESTION: We're thinking of moving to another state to retire. If one of us needed to go on Medicaid, could our move affect the amount of assets retained by the well spouse?

Yes. Before you move, ask your attorney what assets may be kept in each state if there's a medical catastrophe.

HINT: Don't assume that all of the laws and the interpretation of the laws are the same in each state. The key for you is to find an attorney who is knowledgeable in "elder law" in both the state you are living in now and the state you are thinking of moving to.

Nursing home arrangements

QUESTION: I'm about to move to a nursing home. I think my son will handle the paperwork to spare me. Is there anything he or I should be aware of?

Yes. You should know the levels of care being offered in the home. You may only need "custodial care" now. Custodial care essentially means that you are not receiving medical care. If your condition worsens, would you want to stay in the same nursing home? If so, you need to know if the nursing home also offers "skilled care." Skilled care generally involves medical assistance for you.

You should review your nursing home insurance policy to see what types of benefits are covered (for example, skilled care may be covered but you may have no benefits for custodial care under the policy). Check your policy to see if a mental disability such as Alzheimer's is covered.

HINT: Your son should be careful what he's signing at the time you're admitted to the nursing home. It's best to show the paperwork to your attorney before you're admitted. That way your son won't "accidentally" be signing a blank check admission agreement to pay your nursing home bills. The agreement may call your son a "sponsor" but the two of you should be sure that he is not really a guarantor of your bills (unless that's your intent).

Funeral arrangements

QUESTION: When my father died, my mother knew what he wanted in the way of a funeral. Later, when my mother died, we had no idea if she wanted to be cremated like my father. How can I be sure my kids don't go through that agony of trying to know what I had in mind for funeral arrangements?

You need to put your desires in writing. If your will spells out your arrangements and your will is placed in your safe deposit box, it's possible no one may have access to your wishes until after your funeral is over.

So be sure that your loved ones (and executor) know your desires in advance and also whether you have already made arrangements such as prepaying funeral or cremation costs.

HINT: Expressing your desires in writing can avoid family fights or misunderstandings at a time when there is already enough grief to go around for everyone.

See the checklist for funeral arrangements on page 209.

Borrowing against life insurance with a terminal condition

QUESTION: I've just been told that I have six months to live. My condition is terminal. I cannot work and I'm running out of funds. My only asset is a life insurance policy but it only pays off when I die. What can I do?

You should ask your life insurance agent whether you can borrow against your policy now. With AIDS and cancer putting so many people in your position, some states are now allowing you to receive a portion of the death proceeds while you are still alive.

HINT: This will become more and more common over time. Some insurance companies will work directly with you in arranging the advance payment of a portion of proceeds. In other cases, you'll be dealing with third parties. At this very vulnerable time you should protect yourself by having your attorney review the paperwork before you sign anything.

Disability insurance

QUESTION: My husband and I have our own business. We have a seven-year-old daughter. It seems we need every cent we earn to live on. Should we look into disability insurance or is it a waste of money in our case?

Take out a pencil and paper and figure out how your family would survive if you and/or your husband became disabled.

Could you keep your house on one income? Would your daughter be able to go to college? Would there be enough for food on the table on one income?

If you don't have sufficient resources to withstand a disability, you owe it to your daughter to explore the cost and benefits of disability insurance.

HINT: There are ways to minimize disability costs. For example, you could delay the start of benefit payments. It's cheaper to have a policy that only starts paying after you've been disabled for three months as compared to one that starts paying after one month of disability. Of course, you should consider whether a three-month waiting period is feasible for you.

Some policies pay benefits for five years as

compared to paying to age 65. Five years of benefits may not be enough for you.

Also, check into the definition of disability. Are you considered disabled only if you cannot work in your current occupation or only if you can't work in virtually any occupation?

And, finally, these days, you must look into the financial stability of the insurance company insuring your benefits. Will the company be around when you need it?

How to avoid vanishing health insurance

QUESTION: My wife and I are worried about losing our jobs and our health insurance. What can we do to avoid having our health insurance disappear?

You could look into a backup health insurance policy. Because the cost of a full-benefit, major medical health insurance policy is so high, you might instead consider a policy that only pays in the event of a catastrophic illness. Such a policy might have a high deductible such as $15,000. That's no small sum to pay out of pocket, but it might be better to have such a policy than to have no insurance at all.

HINT: Even if you keep your job, this may be a concern. How long will your wife and family get to keep your company benefits if you die while you are still employed by the company?

You should contact an insurance agent and have the agent explain your options to you. You may find such catastrophic insurance through a national charitable support group or an association in the industry in which you work. Sometimes these policies cover you even if you have health problems now if the benefits start after a specified waiting period.

You should also see if your state offers a special
health insurance plan if you are otherwise un-
insurable for health reasons.

Also, you might see whether it makes sense
(economically) for your children to be covered
under their own policies rather than your policy at
work. That way, if something happened to your
job, your children would still have their own
health insurance. Bear in mind, however, if you
select a health plan that only covers or provides
services performed in your home state (as compared to anywhere in the nation), your children
could have a problem if you're forced to move
out of state to look for work.

PART SEVEN

PUTTING
IT ALL
TOGETHER

Putting it all together

QUESTION: There's a lot to read in this book. Can you quickly summarize the big-picture aspects of this book? In other words, what are the main questions I should ask myself?

You need to deal with the following:

WHO
WHAT
HOW
HOW MUCH and
WHEN

If that's *too* brief a summary, then please keep reading.

WHO

Do you have a will or trust that spells out who is going to inherit from you?

Your spouse?

Your children?

Your grandchildren?

Charities?

Who *don't* you want to inherit from you?

Who will manage your assets if you're incapacitated or pass away?

Who will raise your minor children if you die?

Who will inherit your assets after your spouse dies? Can this be changed by your spouse to someone else, such as another spouse?

Have you (or should you) enter into any agreements with co-owners of assets or a business as to what happens upon your death or theirs?

Who will be paying the death taxes on the various inheritances from your estate?

WHAT

What is each beneficiary going to inherit?

What personal items such as furniture and clothing are going to be inherited by which beneficiaries?

What is going to happen to the rest of your assets?

Are your children going to become co-owners of each and every asset you have or are you going to leave certain assets (such as a business) to the one child who works in the business and other assets to other children?

What special arrangements and considerations have you made for certain beneficiaries?

HOW

Will there by a court probate upon your death?

Will at least some of your assets pass to your designated beneficiaries without a court probate upon your death?

HOW MUCH

If your estate will go through probate, what will be the fees for the attorney and executor?

What will the death and other taxes total as a result of your death?

Where will the cash to pay death taxes come from?

Have you taken steps in your estate planning documents to

fully utilize the federal death tax and generation-skipping transfer tax exemption for you (and your spouse if you're married)?

Are there other steps you need to take now regarding title to assets to minimize the amount of future income tax and death tax?

Should you be making gifts now to reduce your estate?

Are you leaving equal or unequal shares to your children?

WHEN

Are assets being left outright to the beneficiaries or placed in trust and paid out over time?

If in trust, for how long and under what conditions are distributions to be made to your beneficiaries?

These are the big picture items to think about.

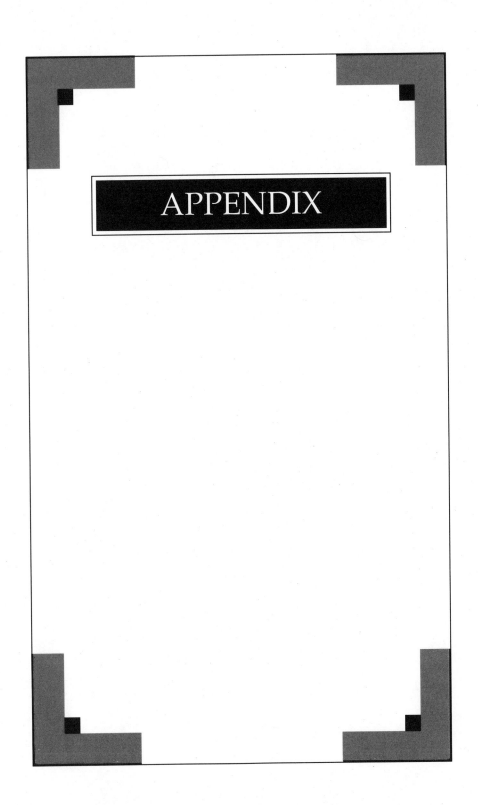

APPENDIX

Federal death tax rates

QUESTION: How is the federal death tax calculated for U.S. citizens and permanent residents?

Net Worth	Amount of Federal Death Tax
$600,000	None
$700,000	$ 37,000
$750,000	$ 55,500
$800,000	$ 75,000
$900,000	$114,000
$1,000,000	$153,000
$1,200,000	$235,000
$1,500,000	$363,000
$2,000,000	$588,000

Above $2,000,000, it's $588,000 plus 50 to 55 percent of the amount above $2,000,000

20 items to keep in your safe deposit box

QUESTION: What should I keep in my safe deposit box?

Here's a list of the top 20:

1. Trusts
2. Wills
3. Powers of Attorney
4. Nominations of Conservator
5. Ownership deeds (i.e., grant deeds) including any documents on cemetery plots or other funeral arrangements
6. Policies of title insurance on real estate
7. Fire, liability and earthquake insurance policies
8. Life, accident, disability and health insurance policies (If you or your executor cannot locate a life insurance policy, a self-addressed, stamped envelope can be sent to American Council of Life Insurance, Lost Policy Department, 1001 Pennsylvania Ave., NW, Washington, DC 20004-2599 and the council will ask its members to do a free search for the missing policy.)
9. Stocks, bonds, promissory notes, trust deeds and credit card information
10. Federal and state death tax and gift tax returns and appraisals done in connection with a death or gift
11. Pension documents
12. Lists of furniture and other personal property of value

plus receipts for improvements to your residence (have photographs and/or camcorder videotapes recorded with a running narrative describing the items and any special characteristics to substantiate greater or lesser than expected value)

13. Automobile ownership certificates
14. Agreements including buy/sell agreements, bills of sale, tax documents and receipts for major purchases
15. Birth, marriage and death certificates, as appropriate, of close relatives
16. Passports
17. Naturalization/citizenship papers
18. Military documents
19. A list of addresses and phone numbers of all persons named as executor, trustee and guardian (have this list at home, too)
20. A list of all of the items in the safe deposit box

Letter of instruction

QUESTION: What would be in a letter of instruction?

Besides having a will or trust, you may want to prepare a letter of instruction to tell your family about matters that aren't covered in your will or trust. If you do write such a letter, have your attorney review an "advance copy" to be sure this "non-legal" document does not conflict with your will and estate planning.

Funeral arrangements

Describe what you want done and where as well as any financial arrangements you've already completed (see the "checklist for funeral arrangements" on page 209)

List of people to be notified

Include the names, addresses and phone numbers of all persons who should be notified about your death.

Guide to locating important papers

See the "location of assets and documents checklists" on pages 224-225 to guide you in stating where you've put important documents (will, trusts, agreements, deeds, promissory notes, etc.)

Trusts – List the name, address and phone number

of the trustee and the type of trust

Assets, liabilities and other documentation

Savings, checking and stock brokerage accounts – List the name of the institution, address and phone number where your account is located, account numbers, type of account(s)

Stock and bond certificates – State where they are located and list the certificate numbers

Life insurance, disability insurance, employee benefits, retirement plans, Keoghs and IRAs - List the source of the benefit including policy numbers, account numbers and beneficiaries (primary and secondary).

Partnerships – State the location of the partnership agreement, name, address and phone number of the general partner(s) and the CPA for the partnership, the type of partnership and your interest in the partnership.

Accounts receivable – Give the name, address and phone number of the person who owes money to you, state the amount owed and the repayment terms.

Small business owned by you – State what should happen to the business. If it's to be sold, list the name, address and phone number of likely buyers, your ranking of the possible buyers, probable sales price and sales terms. If it's to be continued, identify 1) important suppliers and customers to be contacted and what's to be said to them so that the business will continue to operate smoothly, and 2) who in the business should be doing what and 3) who, if anyone, should be brought in to fill your shoes. Possibly a videotape should be made with a camcorder to visually point out certain aspects of the business, products sold, services provided, inventory and manufacturing processes that would be lost without your explanation.

Loans payable – List lender, address and phone number, approximate balance owed, security given for the loan and the repayment terms.

Income tax and gift tax returns (if any) – Indicate the location of all returns and backup information supporting the returns and the name, address and phone number of your CPA.

Real estate – Give the location of your ownership deed, mortgage papers, property tax bills and leases and other agreements and documents (e.g., rent control documents) affecting the real estate.

Cars, trucks and boats – State where the ownership and registration documents are located.

Insurance – Home, medical, liability and other insurance policies – Make a list of the name, address and phone number of the insurance companies, the policy numbers and where the original policies are located.

Credit cards issued to you – List the issuers and card number

Checklist for funeral arrangements

QUESTION: What should I cover in my funeral instructions?

Your direction for funeral arrangements should cover at least the following items:

1. The nature of the ceremony (if any) you want—indicate whether it's to be religious or non-religious, elaborate or private
2. Name, address, phone number and title of person to officiate
3. Location of ceremony
4. Name and location of cemetery
5. Burial or cremation
6. Name, address and phone number of any entity to which you've prepaid for services
7. If burial, location of plot/crypt
8. If cremation, disposition of ashes
9. Headstone/monument requests
10. Donation of body organs

How to save attorney's fees

QUESTION: What can I do to save attorney's fees?

Step ONE: Get organized

The better organized you are before meeting with your attorney, the less time it will take to complete your estate plan. You should have the following ready beforehand:

1. A detailed list of your assets and liabilities.

2. For assets, make copies of documents (such as deeds) showing how title is held.

3. Make a copy of your beneficiary designation forms.

4. Think of the items you want to leave to different individuals including those who would be alternate takers if your first choice did not survive you. Who would be your alternate choice as beneficiary if a beneficiary did not survive you or until the end of a trust?

5. Who would you want to manage your financial affairs while you are alive but incapacitated? Who are your backup choices?

6. Who would you want to manage your assets after you pass away? Who are your backup choices?

7. Who would you want to raise your children?

STEP TWO: Finding the right attorney for you

Once you've thought this through, you may want to talk to friends and relatives to see if they can recommend a good attorney for you.

If you don't want to get these people involved in this matter at all, you might contact the local bar association in your area and ask for a list of estate planning attorneys. You can also ask if they have a special program whereby you can meet with an attorney for a half hour or an hour at a low cost or no charge at all. That way you can interview one or two attorneys to find someone you are comfortable with to discuss and resolve these very personal issues.

Before meeting with the attorney, it's very appropriate to ask how the attorney charges (is it a flat fee, by the hour or a combination approach) and what is the hourly rate for the attorney. Find out what the fees are for office conference time, telephone conference time (including any minimum charges per call) and drafting time. Finally, ask whether there should be separate representation if you are married in order to avoid any conflict of interest. For example, if you have children by a previous marriage, think about the potential for a conflict of interest between your current spouse and your children.

Get organized now!

QUESTION: If I can't make heads or tails of my assets and paperwork, how will my spouse, children or attorney do so if I'm gone?

If you take just an hour to fill out the questionnaire and location of documents forms on the next few pages, you could save your loved ones hours of additional grief and avoid overlooked or lost assets.

List of assets

It's a good idea to make a detailed list of assets and update it each year. A good time to do this is when you are completing your income tax returns.

Make your list in pencil so you can update it annually. It should include names, amounts and account numbers (as necessary) of assets.

On your list of assets, include not only the current fair market value of each asset, but also its value when you acquired it and when and in what state you acquired it. Note your marital status at the time of acquisition and the form of ownership in which you hold title.

List your life insurance policies including company name and policy numbers. Be sure to include not only the face value of your policies but also the cash surrender value and any additional benefits such as for an accidental death.

Safe deposit box

Before it's too late, find out the rules for access to your safe deposit box if you've passed away or are incapacitated.

If you've passed away, there may be a way to allow easy access to your box even if no one else can enter the box while you're alive. You may want to give a completely trusted loved one a key even if you do not put the person on the box as a permitted signer while you are alive. Then, after you pass away, possession of the key and the presentation of your death certificate may permit easy access and avoid unnecessary expenses and delays. (Ask your attorney about the rules in your state.)

Since, in general, there is no registry of wills and trusts, your best bet is to keep a will or trust in your safe deposit box and let the persons named as executor and/or trustee know the location of your safe deposit box. It's also a good idea to advise the executors and trustees of the name, address and phone number of your attorney, CPA, life insurance agent and personal physician, too.

(If you are not married, just fill in the applicable portions)
ESTATE PLANNING QUESTIONNAIRE

TODAY'S DATE:_____

PART I: FAMILY DATA

Information about you

Full name _____ Soc. Sec. # _____

Other or former names _____

Home address _____

Telephone Home (__)_____ Work (__)_____

Birthdate _____ Birthplace _____

U.S. Citizen? ____ Driver's license number _____

Occupation _____

Employer _____

Information about your spouse

Full name _____ Soc. Sec. # _____

Other or former names _____

Home address _____

Telephone Work (__)_____

Birthdate _____ Birthplace _____

U.S. Citizen? ____ Driver's license number _____

Occupation _____

Employer _____

Marital information

When (_____) and where (_____)
were you married?

Children and grandchildren of you and/or your spouse

Have you or your spouse ever had children? ___

Have you or your spouse ever had children from a
    former marriage? ___

Do you or your spouse have any stepchildren now? ___

Do you or your spouse have any foster children now? ___

Do you or your spouse have any other financial dependents?

___

Full names of Children	Living? (Yes/No)	Date of Birth	Married (Yes/No)

If any children are from a prior marriage, indicate which are your children (_____) and which are your spouse's (_____).

Grandchildren

Full names of Granchildren	Living? (Yes/No)	Date of Birth	Names of Parents

Your Parents (P), Brothers (B) and Sisters (S)

Full name	P, B or S	Living? (Yes/No)	City and State

Your spouse's Parents (P), Brothers (B) and Sisters (S)

Full name	P, B or S	Living? (Yes/No)	City and State

Existing wills, trusts and agreements

Do you have a will? ___ If so, what is the date of your will? _____

Are you a beneficiary, trustee, co-trustee or creator of any trust? ____ If so, what is the date of the trust?

_____

Does your spouse have a will? ___ If so, what is the date of your spouse's will? _____

Is your spouse a beneficiary, trustee, co-trustee or creator of any trust? ____ If so, what is the date of the trust?

_____

Have you and your spouse signed a prenuptial or post-nuptial agreement? ___ If so, when? _____

<u>Information about your marriage</u>

List the states/countries in which you have lived during this marriage, including the dates: _____

_____

<u>Information about prior marriages, if any</u>

Have <u>you</u> been married before? ___ How many times? ___

Were the prior marriages ended due to death or divorce?

_____ List the name(s) of your former spouse(s): _____

_____

Has <u>your spouse</u> been married before? ___ How many times? ___

Were the prior marriages ended due to death or divorce?

_____ List the name(s) of the former spouse(s):

_____

<u>Education of your children</u>

Do you have any children in college? Yes __ No __

Do you anticipate sending any children to college in the future? Yes __ No __ Do your children own any assets? Yes __ No If "Yes", how much? _____

PART II: ASSETS AND LIABILITIES

Assets owned by you and/or your spouse

Checking and savings accounts and other

   cash assets $_____

Family business $_____

Stocks and bonds $_____

Jewelry, cars, boats, paintings, clothing,

   furniture, and other personal property $_____

Real property (addresses):

_____ $_____

_____ $_____

_____ $_____

IRAs, Keogh and corporate retirement plans

Type of Plan	Primary Beneficiary	Contingent Beneficiary	Amount

Life and annuity insurance policies

Name of Company	Primary Beneficiary	Contingent Beneficiary	Amount

Trusts from which you benefit $_____

Other assets (partnership interests, patents, etc.) $_____

               Total assets $_____

You and your spouse's liabilities   Amount

Mortgages on real property (addresses)

    _____ $_____

    _____ $_____

    _____ $_____

Car loans $_____

Promissory notes signed by you and/or your spouse $_____

Other debts $_____

Support agreements and other agreements $_____

Other loans and judgments $_____

Guarantees signed by you/your spouse $_____

                        Total liabilities $_____

PART III: INCOME SOURCES AND ADVISORS

	You	Spouse
Annual earned income (salary, etc)	_____	_____
Taxable interest & dividends	_____	_____
Rents	_____	_____
Tax-free income	_____	_____
Total	$_____	$_____

Name of your attorney: Name of your accountant:

_____   _____

Phone:_____   Phone:_____

Name of your insurance agent: Name of your investment
                                advisor:

_____   _____

Phone:_____   Phone:_____

PART IV: HEALTH

Your health status

How is your health? _____. Are there any
conditions to be aware of? ___ If yes, what are they?

_____

Your physician

Please state the name, address and phone number of your
physician _____

Your spouse's health status

How is your spouse's health? _____. Any conditions
to be aware of? ___ If yes, what are they?

_____

Your spouse's physician

Please state the name, address and phone number of your
spouse's physician _____

Health insurance

Do you have health insurance? ___ If so, with what
company? _____

Does your spouse have health insurance? ___ If so, with
what company? _____

If something happened to you or your spouse, would the surviving spouse have adequate health coverage? ___
Would your children have adequate health coverage? ___

Disability insurance

How much disability insurance do you have?

$_____/month until age ___.

How much disability insurance does your spouse have?

$_____/month until age ___.

LOCATION OF
ASSETS AND DOCUMENTS

Note: If something happens to you, how will the important records be located? Will assets be overlooked? Will delays and frustration result from an inability to locate vital records?

Safe deposit box (location, who has access and keys)

_____

Original current will and trusts (location and date)

_____

Life, health and accident insurance policies (location)

_____

Passbooks for savings, CD's checking (location)

_____

Stocks and bonds _____

Income tax returns (location) _____

Contracts and business agreements (location)

_____

Real estate and condominium deeds, title policies and leases

_____

Custody and other managed accounts (location)

_____

Cancelled checks and stubs/years covered (location)

Jewelry and other valuable tangibles (location)

Cemetery plot (location of plot and deed/care arrangements)

Birth certificates _____

Marriage certificates/divorce papers _____

Retirement plan/IRA statements and designations

Military discharge papers _____

Naturalization documents _____

Adoption documents _____

Passports _____

General insurance policies _____

Funeral directions/letter of instructions

Powers of attorney outstanding, including bank accounts and safe deposit box access (dates and names)

Double-checking your Social Security benefits

QUESTION: When I apply for Social Security benefits many years from now, how will I know if my benefits are based on the correct amount of my income through the years?

There is a way.

To keep an eye on the information being used by Social Security, request and complete a Request for Earnings and Benefit Estimate Statement (Form SSA-7004) from Social Security at least every three years. The form is simple to fill out and free.

You will receive both a listing of your earnings (according to their records) and a projection of your Social Security benefits. Then, if there's any mistake in your records, you can have them make a correction before it's too late.

You can order the form by calling 1/800-772-1213.

Umbrella insurance for a rainy day

QUESTION: These days one car accident or a stranger slipping and falling on my front porch can result in a tremendous lawsuit. If my liability insurance coverage is too low, am I putting everything I own on the line every time I step into my car?

This is not a society where people are shy about suing.

The usual amount of car insurance doesn't protect you against the major losses that are so easy to result.

One relatively inexpensive solution is to have "umbrella insurance" on top of your regular car and home liability insurance. This kind of insurance starts paying when your other insurance coverage is exhausted. You may be able to get up to $1,000,000, $2,000,000 or more of coverage for far less than you think.

Ask your liability insurance agent about umbrella insurance. That way you may not get soaked when a bit of rain pours into your life.

Procrastination is your worst enemy!

QUESTION: Am I the only one avoiding the completion of my will?

It appears to be human nature to dread the thought of death.

Remember, if you delay completing your will or trust, what you had in mind won't happen. The results can be tragic.

Your intended beneficiaries may not benefit as much or at all. Death taxes and income taxes paid to the government might be hundreds of thousands of dollars extra or even greater amounts.

Expenses and attorney's fees might be multiplied tremendously.

Why expose your loved ones to all of this? Don't delay. Give yourself a realistic deadline to get started and to finish your will or trust.

Besides making it easier down the line for your loved ones to cope with your passing, you will feel a sense of satisfaction and peace of mind that you have fulfilled one of your responsibilities as a parent or grandparent.

Maybe the best will to leave to your children

QUESTION: What's an ethical will?

It's well and good to be fortunate enough to leave a monetary inheritance to your children.

But the greatest gift you can give to your child or children does not have a monetary value–it has an ethical value. When all is said and done, most of us want ourselves and our children to be good people who make the world a better place.

We don't often take the time to put on paper what values we hold as our ideals. Perhaps the best will to leave to your children is an "ethical will."

Ethical wills date back to biblical times. An ethical will does not have a required format. If you want further direction, there are books written on how to do your own ethical will.

An ethical will often tells your children the values you hold deepest, the most important lessons you've learned in life, your favorite sayings, special family expressions and the religious or secular writings you hold dearest to your heart. You might tell of mistakes you've made and, sometimes, even ask for forgiveness. This might be the time to finish unfinished business.

You can put your ethical will in writing or on a videotape with a camcorder (the lawyer in me does ask that you show your ethical will to your attorney so that this separate document does not contain material that might upset the apple cart of your monetary estate plan).

Tell your children and grandchildren what you value the most. What a shame it would be if you passed on without them knowing this.

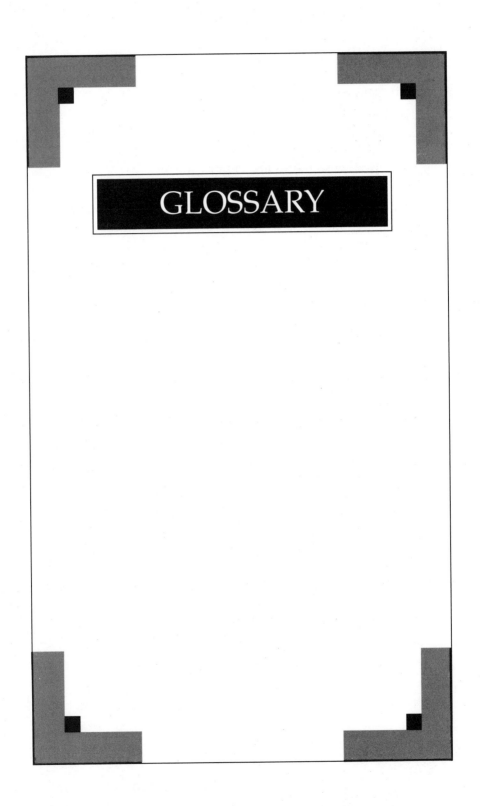

GLOSSARY

A Trust (See Marital deduction)

Basis (See Income tax basis.)

B trust (See Death tax savings trust.)

Charitable remainder trust A special type of irrevocable trust that may allow you to receive income tax deductions now, get tax-free income from the trust and have a charity receive the balance on your death without being subject to death tax.

Codicil An amendment to a will.

Community property A way for married couples to own assets in certain states that may produce income tax and death tax benefits.

Conservator A person appointed by a court to manage your financial and/or personal affairs if you are incapacitated.

Credit shelter trust (See Death tax saving trust.)

Death tax A catch-all term for a variety of federal and state taxes that may be due after a death.

Death tax saving trust A special kind of trust used by the first spouse to die to potentially double the $600,000 exemption from death tax.

Directive to physician (See Living will.)

Discretionary trust A trust in which the trustee has discretion to spend or not spend money of the trust for the beneficiary according to the standards you've set up in the trust document.

Domicile The state where you have your permanent home to which you always intend to return.

Executor The person or entity you name in your will to manage your assets right after you die.

Exemption trust (See Death tax saving trust.)

Family pot trust A type of trust that holds the shares of two or more children in one trust and allows them to benefit as needed (and often unequally) from the assets in the trust.

Generation-skipping transfer tax A special kind of death tax on assets passing to grandchildren or other beneficiaries much younger than you.

Gift tax A catch-all term for a variety of federal and state taxes that may be due whenever you make a gift during your lifetime.

Guardian of the estate A person appointed by a court to manage assets left directly to your children and not in a trust for them.

Guardian of the person A person appointed by a court to raise your child(ren).

Holographic will A handwritten will.

Income tax basis The starting point for calculating income tax gain or loss.

Inter vivos trust (See Living trust.)

Intestate or intestacy Dying without a will.

IRA A type of personal retirement plan known as an "individual retirement account."

Irrevocable life insurance trust A trust that cannot be changed that is used to own life insurance in a way to reduce death taxes.

Irrevocable trust An inflexible, fixed trust–you cannot cancel or change the trust once it's been signed. This type of trust is usually used to make family gifts to reduce death taxes.

Joint tenancy A common way of holding title (ownership) to assets. Joint tenancy assets pass automatically to the surviving joint tenants (co-owners).

Life insurance trust A type of irrevocable trust used to receive life insurance proceeds and keep them out of your estate for death tax purposes.

Living trust (also known as a "revocable trust") A trust that permits you to keep control over your assets while you are alive but helps you avoid probate when you die if certain steps are taken while you are alive.

Living will A "pull-the-plug" document dealing with removal of life support in certain terminal situations.

Marital deduction A special federal tax deduction available to married couples in certain circumstances. Very often, a QTIP trust or a special kind of trust called an "A trust" is used to obtain this deduction.

NAMI (National Alliance for the Mentally Ill) A family-based organization whose purpose is to eradicate mental illness and improve the quality of life of persons suffering from these diseases. NAMI is located at 2101 Wilson Blvd., #302, Arlington, Virginia 22201 (703/524-7600).

Natural death declaration (See Living will.)

Nomination of conservator A document in which you specify the person(s) you want to act on your behalf if you become incapacitated.

Pourover will A special kind of will that is used with a living trust to direct the distribution of certain assets kept outside of the living trust.

Power of attorney for finances A document that allows someone else to manage your finances—it's also often called a "license to steal" since it can be easily abused. If it's a durable power of attorney, it can still be valid after you become incapacitated.

Power of attorney for health care A document by which you appoint an agent to make health care decisions for you. If it's a durable power of attorney, it can still be valid after you become incapacitated.

Probate To some people, it's really a four letter word. Probate is the legal procedure set up by your state to see that taxes, debts and expenses are paid and your remaining assets are distributed to the correct beneficiaries or heirs. This procedure is supervised by a court sometimes referred to as the "probate court." Most people associate higher attorney and executor fees, delays and hassle with probates.

A living trust may avoid probate.

Probate court The name of the court that oversees the administration of estates of deceased persons.

QDOT trust A special kind of trust set up to benefit a surviving spouse who is not a U.S. citizen.

QTIP trust A special kind of trust set up to benefit a surviving spouse by deferring the federal death tax, helping to reduce the generation-skipping transfer tax and maintaining control over the trust after the surviving spouse passes away.

Revocable trust (See Living trust.)

Second-to-die policy A type of life insurance policy that pays the proceeds when both spouses are gone.

Special needs trust A special kind of trust designed to help protect the benefits being received by individuals who are on certain governmental aid programs.

Testamentary trust A trust created under a will.

Testate A person who dies having a will.

Trust A document. Also, a way of leaving assets under a will or living trust with strings attached.

Trustee The person or entity you appoint in your testamentary trust or in your living trust to manage your assets.

Will A document that says who gets your assets after you die.

INDEX